Film Fooled:
An Insider's Guide to the Hilariously Misguided Concept of Film School

by

Seth Hymes

Cover Photograph: Jonathan Wolf
Cover Design: Seth Hymes

ISBN # 978-0-6151-8017-5

Copyright ©2007 Seth Hymes

Contact the author at:

seth.hymes@gmail.com

TABLE OF CONTENTS

FORWARD..5

INTRODUCTION..7

PART I. FRESHMAN YEAR

Chapter 1: Taperecorders &Slideshows 21

Chapter 2: Habitat for the Humanities 31

Chapter 3: Fun with Numbers 47

PART 2. SOPHOMORE YEAR

Chapter 4: The Silent Revolution...…...61

Chapter 5: Sitcoms & Documentaries 70

PART 3. JUNIOR AND SENIOR YEARS

Chapter 6: Method Spending 83

Chapter 7: Producing the $100,000 Short Film............................91

Chapter 8: Working for Free and Paying to Work.......................99

Chatper 9: Salt in the Wounds 109

PART 4. GRADUATION AND BEYOND

Chapter 10: Life in the Inner Circle...125

AFTERWORD 148

Foreword

Investing in college is just like investing in the stock market, with one small difference. While the Security and Exchange Commission enforces the disclosure of potential risks and benefits of any stock or mutual fund to protect investors, no such disclosure is required by colleges.

Unfortunately, there is little to no discussion about the value of a college degree between parents, teachers, and high school students. If you browse the college section at Borders or Barnes and Noble, you will see literally hundreds of guides ranking various college programs, and offering tips on how to gain admission. Students are pressured to take standardized tests like the SATs and enroll in extracurricular activities all to make themselves appear more attractive to potential colleges.

They are then further pressured to taken on the heavy burden of exorbitant student loans, without actually examining the practical benefit of the education.

The majority of students in America today have been led to believe that a Bachelor's Degree is *essential* to launch a successful and fulfilling career. This is not true, but it is perceived to be, which is why young people are under so much pressure to go to college. The truth is that while some employers do prefer to hire college graduates, there are many who do not. A solid work history and good interviewing skills are often enough to get one's "foot in the door". This is true in business, real estate, hospitality, public relations, and many others fields, including film production.

You need only go to www.projectstudendebt.com and click on "voices", then "recent stories" to read many horror stories about graduates deeply mired in tens of thousands of dollars worth of debt, their degrees proving to be absolutely useless in the workplace. A great number of books could be written by people who are in worse situations than me outlining the various shortcomings of their particular programs to prepare them for the realities of the working world.

However, I happened to go to film school at NYU. And it was within the context of this particular program that I experienced a gross disconnect between the reputation of the institution, the quality of the instruction, and the value of the education upon graduation. This disconnect was so vast and bizarre I felt it warranted the writing of an entire book.

I did not write this book to demonize NYU in particular. I actually enjoyed my time there socially. I made some good friends, and I had some interesting and valuable experiences living in New York City. That said, it's not a matter of whether I "like" or "don't like" the school. It's a matter of disclosing detailed information about a very expensive program to prospective students and their parents, so they can make a more informed decision about whether or not to make such a sizeable investment of their own time and money.

Introduction

I applied to NYU Film because I dreamed of writing and directing feature films. Thanks to a fairly advanced A/V program at my high school, I had already written, shot, and edited a number of shorts on video. I'd even shot a couple 16mm silent films at a local community darkroom. I submitted them in my portfolio. The application process was long and stressful. When I learned of my acceptance to Tisch (another name for NYU's Film School), I was so ecstatic that I literally skipped down the halls of my high school with glee.

I already had movie ideas and half written feature scripts that I wanted to develop under the tutelage of more experienced masters. I was ready to get my hands on some film cameras and start planning and shooting. I was ready to rock and roll!

But to my surprise, the program did not rock. It was more like... gently swaying. And then falling down.

I finished NYU with honors in 3 ½ years, won an award or two, but didn't take any upper level film courses. I simply couldn't afford to put in the extra money on top of tuition to pay for the films. I didn't graduate with much of a reel. This seemed kind of strange, since I had just spent 4 years of my life and thousands of dollars to pay for the program.

So instead of making movies, I decided to have some adventures of my own. I worked at Fox News Channel for a while, which was like working on the Death Star. Then I decided to travel. I lived alone in the woods of Northern California and meditated a lot. I went to Massage School. I lived on Maui. I surfed. I slept in my car.

The car was a Nissan Sentra, and I want to hit the TV whenever I see those TV commercials about that guy who says he's going to spend a week living in his Sentra like it's a big deal, because I pulled that off for like 4 months. Maui is the best place to be a beach bum, because they have clean public showers everywhere and the temp never gets below 68 degrees.

My parents were freaked out that I was homeless on an island 5,000 miles away. But I still worked and showered and ate and everything. I was getting great screenplay materials. After a while they would joke around with me about it. They told me they were looking forward to visiting so that they could sleep in the trunk.

I got tired of traveling and ran out of money and returned to my hometown of Rochester, NY. Everywhere I went I would think about filmmaking but I really had no idea how to get work. Or where to begin. I felt stupid and kind of sad that my dream was over.

Then one day I read Robert Rodriguez's "Rebel Without a Crew" and suddenly I felt the life shoot back through my veins. To make a movie *I just had to do it!* I felt like Marty McFly at the Enchantment Under the Sea Dance when his parents finally kiss and he stops fading away and jumps up and finishes up "Earth Angel" on the guitar.

During my time in the woods, I had written a comedy about a guy trying to get to first base. Literally. Mitch is a sweet double major in Optics and Sports Management who sees his love life as a baseball game. Every time he's out with a girl he sees himself as the batter and the girl as the pitcher. But he always ends up striking out or spiking himself. Finally, he enlists the help of his smooth older cousin to become a better "player". He learns how to play it cool and score. But when he meets a girl that he really likes, he has to find out if there's more to love than winning the game.

The script was called "Breaking Balls".

Somehow, the idea came to me after 3 days of intense meditation on an ancient Sanskrit mantra. Surrounded by nothing but wilderness for miles, in the stillness of the natural beauty of Northern California, with the sounds of helicopters searching for pot farms echoing in the distance, I spent 3 days writing down the exploits of a horny college student trying to reconcile his desire to score with the genuine connection he feels for a girl who is slowly but surely becoming his best friend.

Some time later, I was standing near home plate at our hometown's 14,000 seat AAA baseball stadium, directing Doug Spagnola, the wonderful actor I'd cast to play Mitch, on how to properly get hit in the nuts.

Many people helped the shoot happen. I hadn't come this far alone. Not by a long shot.

See the guy holding the furry looking pole? That's Bob Swede, soundman and gaffer extraordinaire.

The people at Frontier Field gave me an amazing deal. For far less than the price of one class at Tisch, I was able to rent this stadium for almost a week:

Along with Doug, the beautiful and talented Ginger Kroll (www.gingerkroll.com) was gracious enough to make the trip upstate as well.

And on top of that, many local movie lovers showed up to be extras, both on the field and in the stands:

I had an amazing professional crew who graciously worked for deferred pay simply because they believed in the project. We shot on true High Def using the Panasonic Varicam, courtesy of the intrepid Bryan Maslin:

www.maslindigital.tv

I actually knew Bryan from high school, when I did paid freelance PA work for this production company. That was long before I had a Bachelor's Degree.

Mark Foggetti has been shooting and directing commercials and features for over 20 years. I contacted Mark because he refinanced his house to make his own movie, "Checkout", a comedy about a dating service run out of a grocery store. The movie was also shot in Rochester and featured Burt Young, the trainer from the "Rocky" movies.

I wanted to learn from someone with that level of commitment to getting a movie made. Mark lent a ton of time and energy to the project, as well as his lights and gaffing equipment. Mark is an incredible Director of Photography. That's him, looking focused in the center of the frame.

Ryan Cahill, the 21 year old Assistant Director, ran the set with the confidence of a skilled veteran. Ryan kept the 100 plus extras in the stands focused, laughing, and happy for OVER 6 HOURS each night. None of the extras were paid or fed, they were just great sports. Try finding that kind of commitment in LA!. Here's Ryan clutching his megaphone:

We even found a way to get aerial photography for next to nothing, thanks to Craig Shaw of www.stratus-imaging.com. Craig and his brother have this 16 foot helium blimp equipped with a video camera that they operate via remote. Check it:

We floated it over Frontier Field one night and captured this:

As we began shooting, many figures floated through my mind. The ideal budget for the movie was $190,000. With some more favors and profit splitting, we could get it done for $100,000.

I checked my savings account. It did not contain one hundred and ninety thousand dollars. So I set about fundraising. In the legal documents necessary to receive money from private investors, we stipulated a "minimum budget". This was the least amount of money we had to raise before we could start spending the investment capital. It was the very least amount of money we felt necessary to realistically complete the movie.

I believe that figure was somewhere around $80,000.

However, in private conversations with my crew, I knew that if worst came to worse, they would be willing to lower their day rates even more in exchange for a part of any potential profits the movie might make when it got distribution. With that factored in, I knew we could eek the movie out for around $50,000.

$190,000. $100,000. $80,000.

$50,000.

Fifty thousand dollars. Just fifty thousand dollars.

Where had I seen that figure before?

NYU Office of Financial Aid

Office of Financial Aid • New York University

home > tuition, fees, and expenses > tisch undergraduate students

Tuition, Fees, and Expenses

Tisch School of the Arts
Undergraduate Students
2007-08 School Year

The preliminary* budget below approximates the cost of education for the academic year and includes an amount for tuition and fees (depending on the course load); an allowance for room and board (which varies according to where the student lives); a standard amount for books, supplies, and personal expenses; and a transportation allowance.

Budget Components	Commuter Student	Off-Campus Student	On-Campus Student
Tuition and fees (two semesters full-time)	$38,722	$38,722	$38,722
Room and board	$1,480	$11,850	$11,780
Books and supplies	$700	$700	$700
Transportation	$480	varies	varies
Personal expenses	$500	$1,000	$1,000
Total budget	**$41,882**	**$52,272**	**$52,202**

* Estimated at time of publication (March 2007)

Part 1: The Freshman Year

During your Freshman Year at NYU, you will not touch a film or video camera. You will not write a script. Because, you see, you are not ready to make a film. You are but a lowly freshman. You do not understand sound, or images. Hence, you must take a course called "Sound Image". You do not understand the film frame. Or sequence. Hence, you must take a course titled "Frame and Sequence".

I know, you may have even submitted a completed film or video in your portfolio to gain admission to the school. You may have been operating a video or film camera all throughout high school, own your own Final Cut pro editing system, and shot a dozen or more short movies.

But you aren't ready. Trust us.

Film is a delicate art that requires years of practice and mentorship from highly skilled artisans, like our accomplished faculty. Never mind people who didn't attend or complete film school, like the guys who made "South Park" or Hal Ashby or Kevin Smith or Robert Rodriguez or Steven Spielberg or David Fincher or P.T. Anderson or James Cameron or Quentin Tarantino or Woody

Allen or Peter Jackson or Ben Younger or Billy Wilder or Judd Apatow or Stanley Kubrick or Sergio Leone or John Ford or Christopher Nolan or Wolfgang Petersen or Sydney Pollack or Sir Carol Reed or Douglas Sirk or Mel Brooks or Steven Soderbergh or Richard Donner or Blake Edwards or Victor Fleming or John Frankenheimer or Milos Forman or Mike Figgis or Michael Apted or John G. Avildsen ("The Karate Kid") or Wes Craven or Michael Bay or Jonathan Demme or Michael Mann or Guy Ritchie or Danny Boyle or John Sayles or David O. Russell. Or pretty much anyone who made a movie before the 1960, when there was no such thing as film school.

You need film school. As a member of the MTV generation, you have been inundated with visual narratives since your birth. You are skilled in the use of some of the most advanced technical equipment ever invented to capture and manipulate images, like digital video cameras and editing equipment.

And that is why, for your freshman year, we are going to let you play with a tape recorder and make a slideshow.

Chapter 1

Tape Recorders & Slideshows

Course Description:

Digital Frame & Sequence

H56.0039   Studio   4 Credits

Course Level: Introductory

This core production course is to be taken as a complement to Sound Image, in preparation for the Fundamentals of Sight and Sound: Film and Video courses. The course encompasses the basic elements of 35 mm still photography and multi-image sequencing. Covered are all camera functions, depth of field, motion, portraiture, lighting, color, narrative structure, and composition. Sequencing of images is accomplished digitally using Final Cut Pro on Macintosh workstations. The class meets each week during one lecture section for production information, screenings, and discussions along with a lab section where students learn digital editing. Each student does photographic assignments and directs two multi-image projects. Additionally, students serve on a group project. All students must have a 35 mm, fully adjustable camera and light meter. An automatic camera is not acceptable. The light meter may be in the camera. Special Note: Students are expected to put in 12 hours of crewing on upper classmen's film projects to introduce them to this very important collaborative aspect of the film and television profession. During the Freshman Colloquia, upper classmen will pitch their projects for interested students to sign up.

Frame and Sequence is a mandatory, $4,592 photography class. (4 credits at $1,148 a credit = $4,592). I took a Basic Photo class in high school and learned all about depth of field, motion, portraiture, lighting, color, and composition. You can get this from any course at a community darkroom for well under a thousand dollars.

But the teaching of narrative structure is a different animal altogether. For weeks, you will immerse yourself in the craft of weaving a complex and intelligent narrative under the tutelage of a seasoned veteran of the trade. The class is so engrossing, so stimulating that you may lose track of time and space, completely absorbed in creative rapture.

Okay, no. You don't get that. But you will learn about early pinhole cameras.

The course description is almost exactly the same as it was back when I took it back in 1996. This indicates that the administration has clearly taken the many student complaints about the uselessness of the class into serious consideration.

When I went, you had 4 projects. The first one was freestyle, take pictures of what you want. (What guidance!) The second was a PORTRAIT. So I took pictures of my friend Sarah looking sexy and pouty. (Spellbinding!) The third project was with a group (almost like a "crew"!). And the fourth project was not just an exercise. No, for the fourth project you actually got to create a NARRATIVE. A "story" told with pictures. And... music!

A slideshow!

For my final project, I literally brought in a bunch of slides, loaded them into a slide projector, and synched them up with an audio tape. It was fine for presenting to the class. When my parents asked me to show them what I had just done with my first semester of college, all I could do was show them the slides. They were supportive, albeit confused. Like me, they didn't really get it but they assumed the school knew what it was doing.

Nowadays, you don't have to use an actual slide projector. You get to show your projects on a "computer". The course description says that your highly skilled professor will teach you digital editing. How you are supposed to learn editing with still pictures, I don't know. It's not really an accurate description of the class.

When I attended school back in 1996, computer editing technology was still relatively new. The only system available was the AVID, and one of those could cost you $30,000 to $75,000.

Today, most students who attend film school have their own Macintosh or PC computers with non-linear editing software. Video editing has become so affordable that many high schools have their own "video labs" featuring rows of iMacs equipped with iMovei and Final Cut Pro.

The 10th Floor of Tisch features the same Macintosh computers available at Brighton High School, my alma matter. The only difference is that the computers at Tisch are housed inside a building bearing a flag that says "NYU", on Broadway in New York City.

Any high school senior at Brighton can shoot and edit a short film or video. But if you're a Frosh at NYU Film... you can't. But hey, its only the first semester. Next semester, they've got to let you make a film.

Right?

Sound Image

H56.0048   Studio   4 Credits

Course Level: Introductory/Fundamental

Required of all Freshmen and all **radio majors.**

A fundamental-level core production workshop introducing the world of sound in film, television, and radio. Students will explore through individual and group projects of increasing complexity and sophistication the art of creating a "theater of the mind" in the sound medium.

Laboratory periods are designed to provide a wide variety of audio recording experiences both on location and in studio. Specific production techniques such as live recording, mixing, and editing will be stressed.

Lectures will focus on the theories of basic acoustics and audio electronics, the aesthetics of the sound medium, and the development of critical listening skills.

Sound Image is a great class to take if you have a keen interest in Radio. After all, you spend a lot of time in Radio Booths, using the same mics they use in Radio, and for your final project, you will produce a full length Radio Drama. The course was originally offered exclusively for Radio Majors, working in the Radio Department, who were attending Radio School so they could have an exciting career in the exciting world of Radio.

So naturally, the course is mandatory for Film and TV Majors.

When I took Sound Image long ago, the course description was about the same as you see it listed above. But we didn't learn a thing about feature film sound recording. We learned about Radio recording.

If you've ever seen a film set portrayed in popular culture, you will notice that all of the microphones are long and elliptical. Like a shotgun. Hence, these mics are called "shotgun" mics. These mics are so named because due to their streamlined shape, they only pick up sound in the direction they are facing. Hence, the technical name "uni-directional". These mics are used for dialogue so that, in a crowded marketplace, you only hear what your actors are saying and not the curious musings of Achmad the Grocer, standing 10 feet to the left of your star.

Shotgun mics are the most common mics used in the movies.

But, in this fundamental course, we didn't even touch a shotgun microphone. Nor did we deal with dialogue in a scene.

Instead, when I took this class, we were given an audio tape recorder that must have been manufactured in the late sixties. It was a bulky, clunky, metallic device with an omni directional microphone. ("Omni directional" microphones pick up sound from all over the place. They are rarely used in movies.)

We were told to go out into the city and "record sounds".

So we did. Sounds of the subway. Sounds of traffic. Sounds of the deli down the street.

Then, we came into the class room and listened to these tape recordings, and tried to figure out where they were taken.

"Did you take this in the subway?" I asked, listening to the roar of the train.

"Why yes!" my classmate answered, his mouth agape. "How-ever-did-you-know?"

It was all part of teaching us about the mysterious "theater of the mind", and imbuing us with "Critical listening skills".

To be fair, I did find a good use for these Critical Listening Skills. I used to them to detect the sound of all my money being sucked out of my pockets. SSSSWWWWSSSSHHHHHH. Too bad that, at the time, I thought it was the subway.

What followed was a very bizarre semester. We were given further assignments to record sounds. Then, we were given some pseudo-narrative assignments, where were allowed to write short 3 minute radio sketches. We could use actors and sign out these small "radio" booths on the Sound Floor. We recorded sound onto ¼", reel to reel magnetic tape and edited our little projects by literally *cutting the magnetic tape with a razor blade and splicing it together with scotch tape*.

I made a short sketch about Marilyn Manson singing to a bunch of pre-schoolers. It was fun. Don't know what I can do with it. People in the industry aren't usually interested in audio only projects presented on ¼" magnetic tape.

For our final project, we were grouped into teams of 4. I wrote a 10 page Radio Drama called "Delusions of Grandeur", about a guy who gets hit on the head and thinks he is in the movie "Double Indemnity". It won us the Tony Hawkins Award for Excellence in Sound. That was neat, but I still didn't get why I was just about to complete my Freshman Year at the most prestigious school in the country, and all I had to show for it was a slide show and a Radio Drama.

Ross and Craig, the technical wizards on my crew, had taught themselves how to use Pro-Tools, which is a professional audio mixing program. We did all of our editing on a computer (which we had to fight to get permission for). Our unfortunate classmates had to splice their projects together using scotch tape and razor blades.

The school has finally upgraded their technology so that all sound editing is done using Pro Tools. And instead of those clunky audio tape records, students are given Digital Mazer recording units with Flash cards. It sounds fancy, but it's really just a digital tape recorder. And you're still using omni-dimensional mics. And doing radio dramas.

And when did they upgrade from analog tape with razor blades and scotch tape to digital? In 2003.

That's **Seven years** after I took the class, and my intrepid classmates used Pro-Tools.

Seven years.

Jesus.

Baking the Cake

Rather than making tape recordings of sounds of the city with microphones that have nothing to do with feature film sound production, why not take out a $2,000 Sennheiser MKH60 microphone from your local rental house for $100 a week and play with the levels? You could plug the mic into the $3,000 Panasonic DVX-100A Digital Video camera that you purchased with all the money you saved by skipping these two Freshman courses.

Read a book on the subject, then go get on a film set. Bug the sound guy. Watch him. Ask questions. Offer to hold the boom pole. You'll learn more in one day than you will during the entire semester.

It boggles my mind how removed from reality the Administration must be to continue requiring this class. Remember in "The Karate Kid" when Mr. Miyagi made Daniel-San do all of those seemingly irrelevant menial chores around the house, but he was actually learning karate?

I think the Administration thinks they are Mr. Miyagi, and they are teaching students like Daniel-San. But these sound exercises are not like "wax on, wax off". It's more like if Mr. Miyagi told Daniel-San to bake a cake.

And then when it came time to fight Johnny at the tournament, Daniel-San would be dead. He trusted his Sensei to teach him Karate, but all he learned how to do was bake a fucking cake. So now Johnny is attacking him with roundhouse kicks and all Daniel-San can do is to pretend he is mixing cake batter.

If you're on a feature film set and you need to help out with sound recording or boom pole operation, you're clueless. You don't know anything about room tone or sound directionality or mixing or riding levels or gain or operating the appropriate equipment. You're standing there with a digital tape recorder and an omni directional microphone and your radio drama. Your cake. This course has taught you nothing at all. And you've paid $25,000 for the semester.

Beginning Basics

According to the school's own marketing material, the Freshman Year is called "Beginning Basics". Seriously. Like kindergarten. This might have made sense back in 1980, in the school's heyday. Before video cameras and computers with non linear editing systems were readily available at Wal Mart.

It does make sense, but only from the school's point of view. Without stretching out the relatively basic craft of filmmaking over 4 costly years, the school would make no money.

To even get into the school, most students demonstrate an aptitude that exceeds the teachings of the first year curriculum. Most submit a completed video, edited with nonlinear computer based equipment, for their portfolio. Students who have never made a film or video are allowed to submit writing samples or still photos. If a student has never shot a video, why not allow them to dive right in and get their hands dirty with some basic video equipment? It's certainly cheap enough these days. And if they've already worked with video, why not help them refine their skills?

But instead, these talented, driven, creative young people spend an entire year of school playing with irrelevant sound equipment and taking still photographs for the same price as a high grade industrial film camera.

You can get the real basics of filmmaking very inexpensively. You can learn them from another filmmaker, or a book, or a class at a community college. You can just fool around with the camera yourself. Or go to http://acceptable.tv/tutorials and watch their tutorials. Not only are they amusing and informative, but they feature Jack Black(!)

I taught myself how to edit with AVID and Final Cut Pro in under a week. You can too. It's just like word processing with pictures. It's not rocket science.

It is the practice, refinement, and application of those skills that takes time and effort. You should not trust any person or institution who tells you that learning the fundamentals of the filmmaking process require years of academic training or thousands and thousands of dollars.

Let me give you an example. Here is a simple rule of composition to make your work more professional. We call it the one third rule. Divide your frame up with imaginary lines into thirds. Then, frame your subject in either the left third or the right third, *not* the middle.

Like this:

Guy holding a wheel of cheese framed poorly.

Me looking awesome with the 1/3 rule

See? It's simple. This technique can drastically change the appearance of the images you capture, helping to differentiate your work from the average dreck on Youtube. But let's face it, learning and grasping a technique like this is not the same as earning a degree in medicine, engineering, or the law. You can't become a lawyer by reading handy tips in books written by disgruntled law school grads. You have to study detailed, specific, and necessary information. You have to graduate from an accredited school and pass a state mandated exam.

Is all that fuss necessary to reframe your subject and know where to put the lights?

Nope.

Of course, how could anybody truly deliver on a class that costs $4,000+? Outside of an academic setting, no fool in their right mind would pay that much for a class unless it was being taught by Spielberg himself. And, last time I checked, Spielberg never went to film school, much less taught there.

Chapter 2
Habitat for the Humanities

According to a recent survey, NYU is the #1 Dream School for most high school seniors in the U.S. At least, this is what the school told me in its latest request for money. Clearly, NYU's multi **billion** dollar endowment is not enough. To keep its doors open, the school relies on donations from graduating students like me. Kind of like Public Radio.

So many young people dream of paying $42,000 a year in tuition to learn nothing of discernable practical value. Alumni giving helps provide prospective students with scholarships and grants, so that they won't have to resort to organ harvesting to pay for school.

And they make it so easy to give. Take a look at this stylish flyer, which I recently received in the mail.

I Wish to Make a Gift of:

☐ $100   ☐ $1,000   ☐ $10,000
☐ $250   ☐ $2,500   ☐ $25,000
☐ $500   ☐ $5,000   ☐ Other $_____

Please Apply My Annual Fund Gift as follows:

You can provide **General Support** to help recruit and retain top faculty, enhance the quality of campus life, expand internship and mentoring programs, and improve and upgrade our facilities, as well as support for **Scholarship & Financial Aid**.

(Check the box beside the name(s) to which you wish to direct your donation)

	General Support	Scholarship/ Financial Aid
☐ College of Arts and Science	$_____	$_____
☐ College of Dentistry	$_____	$_____
☐ College of Nursing	$_____	$_____
☐ Courant Institute	$_____	$_____
☐ Gallatin School of Individualized Study	$_____	$_____
☐ General Studies Program	$_____	$_____
☐ Graduate School of Arts and Science	$_____	$_____
☐ Heights Arts	$_____	$_____
☐ Heights Engineering	$_____	$_____
☐ Institute of Fine Arts	$_____	$_____
☐ School of Continuing and Professional Studies	$_____	$_____
☐ School of Law	$_____	$_____
☐ School of Medicine	$_____	$_____
☐ School of Social Work	$_____	$_____
☐ Steinhardt School of Culture Education, and Human Development	$_____	$_____
☐ Stern Graduate School of Business	$_____	$_____
☐ Stern Undergraduate School of Business	$_____	$_____
☐ Tisch School of the Arts	$_____	$_____
☐ Wagner Graduate School of Public Service	$_____	$_____
☐ Athletics/Violet Booster Club	$_____	$_____
☐ Friends of Bobst Library	$_____	$_____
☐ Other _____	$_____	$_____

0000607180   UPP07   10-58002
Mr. Seth Hymes
1731 North Normandie Avenue, Apt. 19
Los Angeles, CA 90027

Please make any changes to your personal information above.

☐ Enclosed is my check for $_____ payable to New York University.

☐ I am using my credit card to make this gift of $_____

☐ AmEx   ☐ Visa   ☐ MasterCard   ☐ Discover

Name on Card _____
Card No. _____
Exp. Date _____
Signature _____
E-mail Address _____

Matching Gifts

You may double or triple the value of your gift to NYU if your company has a Matching Gift Program. Visit **www.matchinggifts.com/nyu** for a list of participating companies, and check with your human resources office for more details.

☐ Enclosed is my/my spouse's corporate matching gift application form.

Company Name _____

Please reply using the enclosed envelope or mail to:

New York University
The Fund for NYU
PO Box 837
New York, NY 10009-9984

You can also call 1-800-NYU-4144 between 9:00 AM and 5:00 PM Eastern Time, M-F, to make your gift by credit card, or you can make your gift on-line at **www.nyu.edu/alumni/giving**.

Recognizing Leadership in Giving

❧ **President's Cabinet** $25,000 AND ABOVE
❧ **President's Circle** $10,000 – $24,999
❧ **President's Council** $5,000 – $9,999*

We encourage you to contribute at the leadership level. For all alumni who contribute $5,000 and up, the University recognizes the special value of your gift through Presidential giving clubs. Members are invited to an annual recognition reception with President Sexton and other special university events.

Recent graduates can join **The Young Alumni Leadership Circle** by making a gift of $250-$1,000. The Circle brings together a network of young professionals and recognizes their commitment to NYU.

*Classes of 2002-2006 can also join the President's Council with a minimum gift of $1,000. Classes of 1997-2001 are invited to join with a minimum gift of $2,500.

For further information, contact the Director of The Fund for NYU at (212) 998-6851 or **thefund@nyu.edu**.

Gifts to **New York University** are tax deductible.

Gift Planning

Please send me information about:

☐ Making a gift of appreciated securities or other assets
☐ Naming NYU in my will
☐ How I can make a gift that will pay me income

You can find more information at: **www.nyu.edu/alumni/giving** and click on "Planned Giving" or contact Alan Shapiro, Esq., Director of Gift Planning, at (212) 998-6960 or **alan.shapiro@nyu.edu**

NEW YORK UNIVERSITY
25 West 4th Street, 4th floor
New York, NY 10012-1119
Phone: (212) 998-6851
Fax: (212) 995-4020
www.nyu.edu/alumni/thefund

Apparently, the school gauges one's value as a leader in terms of how much money you can give them. Thank God I don't actually have to do something of merit with my life. All they want is a check, and they'll call it "Recognizing Leadership in Giving". For $5,000 I could be on the President's Council. But that's small potatoes. To buy my way into his *Cabinet*, I need to give them $25,000. And that's what I'm working towards. I've been saving for years to get a legitimate audience with the President, since his office never listened to my concerns when I was just a student.

I noticed there's no way to make a donation to improve the campus housing. But why should there be? This is one area where NYU really does seem to have done it right.

All in all, the school offers a fantastic deal. Students are not only afforded a top notch education, but they are also granted the privilege of inhabiting some of the University's prestigious and spacious dormitories, many of which are built from the finest cinder block in the world. To help cope with cold, New York winters, students will share a small bedroom. The close proximity not only encourages socialization but also increases gross body heat output, saving the school money on heating bills. And that savings is passed right on to the students.

For only about $1500 a month (for each student), you get to share a room the size of crawl space for Chinese refugees. Check out these handsome digs, taken right from NYU's own website:

Rubin Bedroom

Plus you get to share your bathroom with 3 to 5 other guys. Kind of like summer camp, or the Warsaw Ghetto. And there's no kitchen. But why would there be when you can treat yourself to the University's fabulous dining hall food?

I don't know, maybe I'm too old to know what constitutes a "dream school". My dreams tend to involve supermodels and mansions, not this:

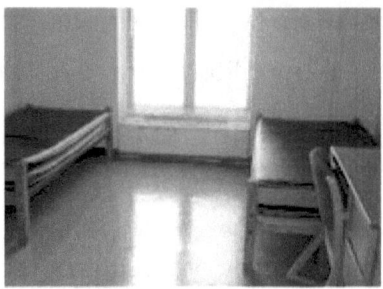

Weinstein Dorm Room

Tisch Core Curriculum

Art in the World (Fall)

The World through Art (Spring)

Required for all Freshmen, Fall and Spring semesters.

The Tisch School of the Arts Core Curriculum began in the Fall of 2001 and was developed for all incoming undergraduate students as a way for students to have a common experience and to integrate students' various professional interests. The courses mix different artistic media, and combine practical and theoretical approaches to achieve a comprehensive grasp of the work that art can do in the world.

The Core Curriculum is required of all Freshmen and fulfills their Expository Writing requirement (transfer students will be evaluated as to whether or not they have previously fulfilled their writing requirement upon receipt of their final transcript). The Core Curriculum consists of two courses - *Art in the World* offered in the Fall semester and *The World Through Art* offered in the Spring semester. All incoming Freshmen must take both semesters. Each course consists of a plenary lecture given by a Tisch Senior Faculty member that meets once a week and a workshop that meets twice a week for both Fall (*Writing the Essay*) and Spring (*Writing the World*) semesters. These writing courses are intensive, interdisciplinary and collaborative. Lectures and workshops focus on how to read complex texts for an understanding of their arguments, and how to write well-reasoned essays supported by evidence. These courses are designed to foster an appreciation of how arts relate to each other and to society in a changing world. These courses will allow students to reflect on a range of social and ethical issues as they pertain to their own creativity.

Related Links

- Art & Public Policy Web Site
- Art and Public Policy Courses
- Minor in Art and Public Policy

Info
Department of Art & Public Policy
665 Broadway, 6th Floor
New York, NY 10012

"Intellectual Masturbation 101"

"Beware of all arts degrees" – Old Klingon Proverb

Imagine your first film related job out of film school. It will more than likely happen 6 to 9 months after you graduate, because by then you will have sent out at least 100+ resumes. You will have already worked in a non film related field to pay the bills... waiting tables or temping, because even the lowest level jobs in the biz are really, really hard to get. Even for film school grads.

Once you do get that break, it will be more than likely be an entry level job on a feature or TV production, or at a post house or a casting agency. You will be answering phones, scheduling appointments, running errands. You will be making coffee. You will be typing, picking up people's lunches. You may be reading shitty scripts and giving your college educated opinion (called "coverage").

You may even be building your resume by doing sound recording or gaffing or being a PA on a small indie movie working for little or no pay.

You try to draw on the knowledge you acquired at school to help you navigate your new job. You remember yourself sitting in a classroom, listening to a lecture. You are dozing off, because you came here to make movies, and for some reason an old guy in a tweed suit is talking to you about the history of Art in the World.

And the World in Art.

It's your 14th hour of holding a boom pole. Or your boss has just yelled at you because you got the Dulce de Leche Frappuccino® Blended Coffee and not the Dulce de Leche Frappuchino® Blended Crème he wanted. Or you're going blind from data entry. Or you've got to run some tapes from Santa Monica to Hollywood in under 2 hours, even though it's 4 PM and rush hour has just begun.

You're being paid minimum wage.

But hey, at least you can write a well reasoned essay.

When I attended the program way back in 1996, these two classes did not exist. I took two semesters of "Expository Writing", which we freshmen affectionately nicknamed "Suppository Writing". It was basically a rehash of everything I learned in 12th Grade English. But it cost more. And I was being taught by nervous Grad Students. And it had nothing to do with Filmmaking.

As enrollees of the NYU Undergrad Film Program, you are subjecting yourself to taking 48 credits worth of non film related courses. They are known as Liberal Arts, or General Education, courses. This is how you earn your Bachelor's Degree.

A Bachelor's Degree is an 18 by 15 inch piece of paper with some calligraphy on it that you can frame on your wall next to your Metallica posters. You can also make mention of it at the bottom of your resume, underneath your work experience.

Your Bachelor's Degree will be worth very little, unless it happens to be printed on material made from Justin Timberlake.

Visualize this degree as you take the various Science, History, English, and Film History Classes necessary to receive the degree.

For my science requirement, I took a class called "Sound and Music". For my troubles, I got to listen to a 60 year old Hungarian Immigrant mumble about sine waves for 4 months. I couldn't understand a word the man said. I had to refer back to my AP Physics notes from high school to pass the class.

Today, this class would cost you $4,592.

For the Film History requirements, I took a class called "Silent Cinema". We watched Silent Movies for 5 months. Because there was no sound, most of the class would fall asleep. It's really hard to watch a movie with no sound. Then there was "Hollywood and Its Alternative", essentially a history class about the old studio system. After I graduated, I learned the same facts watching a great documentary about the subject on A&E. Then, I took a class called "Italian Cinema". I listened to an Italian Professor, watched Italian movies, and I wrote essays about Italian themes, full of Italian bullshit (*sandeces*). Finally, I took a class called "Comparative Directors: Spielberg, Altman, and Coppola." I watched "Jaws" for the 12 millionth time, along with "Apocalypse Now" for the 100th time and "M*A*S*H" for the 3rd time. Then I wrote a paper comparing the three.

The total cost of these four classes, in modern tuition and adjusted for 2007 inflation, is $18,000.

IMAGINE PAYING EIGHTEEN THOUSAND DOLLARS TO WATCH MOVIES.

That's like paying for 83 years of Netflix up front, and only getting a couple dozen movies.

"But aren't the insights of the professors worth the cost?"

Excuse me for a moment. I'm getting a shovel.

Meet the Faculty

You've probably heard some prestigious names associated with NYU Film. Martin Scorsese. Oliver Stone. Spike Lee. And Martin Scorsese. A few famous men who graduated from the Graduate program 25+ years ago when the program cost well under $5,000 and there was no such thing as a camcorder have become the definitive reason why you should spend $200,000 to attend the Undergraduate program today. Sounds reasonable to me.

If you do go to NYU Film, be prepared to hear the names of these men invoked frequently and vigorously in the same manner that George Bush invokes "September 11th" to justify policies and programs that, at first glance, might appear be to unbelievably stupid. After all, even though Freshman year is pointless and costs you more than a down payment on a house... Scorsese went here. (Kind of.)

Lo the school's entire reputation may rest on the laurels of these famous men, it brings to the inquiring mind one question:

What of the *professors*?

Shouldn't the people who actually *teach* the classes, rather than a few famous alumni, be the soap box upon which the school can boast its merit, and upon which hang the metaphorical lapels of its sterling reputation?

I would have thought so. But too often, these wise sages are overlooked for more well known mascots. In my naivety, I thought that the collective works of the faculty of what is considered to be one of the most prestigious film schools in the nation would be widely known and highly regarded.

But alas, it is not so.

As I peruse the school's current web site, I notice that more than half of the faculty listed are credited for documentary work. Such was the case even when I attended the program. And this is natural. After all, what young person attending film school doesn't dream of being the next Errol Morris, Albert Maysles, or Barbara Kopple? Who didn't submit their application fee with fantasies of making the next "Vernon, Florida", "Monterey Pop", "Hear No Evil", or "Harlan County USA"?

Personally, I was inspired by Octavio Getino and Fernando E. Solanas' 1968 masterpiece "La Hora de los Hornos". What I originally thought was going to be a searing European porno turned out to be a searing South American documentary. (Fun fact: in Spanish, "horno" means "furnace").

Clearly, these are the kinds of filmmakers and movies young people have in mind when they apply to film school. I know I did. I didn't apply to film school because I wanted to make the next "Pulp Fiction", "Clerks", or "Die Hard". Heavens no. My dream was to make obscure documentaries limited to discussion in academic circles. Much like the accomplished but underappreciated faculty of Tisch.

It is a sad commentary on our superficial society that most people have never heard of anything done by a majority of the Tisch professors. Even worse, some professors received accolades for their achievements back in the 70s and 80s, and have not done much since. This is a tragedy, because it means that today's incoming freshman may be unfamiliar with their work.

Sure, Spike Lee sometime teaches in the Graduate Department. And the Undergrad faculty does feature the screenwriter of "Wildcats", the cinematographer of "Ernest Saves Christmas", and the editor of "Eight Men Out".

But since society has neglected to acknowledge the work of these esteemed (Martin Scorsese) filmmakers, I have taken it upon myself to share some of their profound accomplishments.

Did you know that it was a Tisch professor who directed Shawn Colvin's riveting music video "Steady On"? This song reached #30 on the Adult Contemporary Charts back in 1990. Oh yes. A Tisch Professor also directed the documentary "Out of Rock, Sing a Song of Children." Some of the other notable Tisch Profs include:

- The Producer/Director of "Spheroid Memories" - a half hour fine arts video essay on the global journey of the world renown artist and performer, Angel Orensanz.

- An elected Chevalier in the Order of the Palmes Academiques by the prime minister of France. This Prof was also the 1998 recipient of the NYU Distinguished Teaching Medal.

- A Screenwriter who has worked with the noted, prize winning Hungarian directors: Zoltan Fabri, Karoly Makk and Marta Meszaros.

- The Producer of Cable Ace Award Winner for Best Music Special, Child of Mine: "Songs To Our Children"

- A recipient of the James L. Hearst Guest Lecturer Award in the Arts and Humanities at the University of Northern Iowa.

- A former President of the University Film and Video Association

- A filmmaker who in 1996 had a one-hour long video documentary, *That Old Gang of Mine*, broadcast on (Public Television) Thirteen/WNET. Also a key participant on the First World Order Project, a long-term telecommunications project that will focus on traditional as well as contemporary expressions of African cultural practice throughout the Americas, the Caribbean, Europe, India, and the Pacific Islands.

- The Project director of *SoundPlay*, the first yearlong nationally distributed series of one-hour radio dramas since 1975, which included the SoundPlay Hörspiel series of German radio dramas and originally commissioned work from American artists and writers

- The screenwriter of "Rocket Gibraltar", "Port of Call", "The Golden Eagle", "Mrs. Dogg", "Paint it Black", "Caught in a Whirlwind", and "Beach House"

In addition, many of the Professors even have Master Degrees and Doctorates from *other* prestigious educational institutions like Harvard and Yale. And as we all know, doing doctoral research, sitting in classrooms, consulting with advisors, and writing long winded academic papers are the essential ingredients of good filmmaking.

But there is one film I was exposed to at film school that I will never forget. It is a film of such brilliance and singular vision that, even today, I find myself at a loss for words when trying to adequately express its magnificence.

That film is, of course is "C.H.U.D. 2: Bud the Chud."

For those of you unfamiliar with the term, C.H.U.D. stands for "Cannibalistic Humanoid Underworld Dweller". The original "C.H.U.D." was a 1984 B-Horror flick about mutant underground vagrants who kill people.

Then, in 1989, somebody felt it was time to make a sequel. But this time, the filmmakers opted for a more lighthearted interpretation of the concept, as illustrated in this summary taken from Rottentomatoes.com:

"When a trio of friends snooping at the school science lab discover a corpse and accidentally let it roll away, they need a replacement fast. They find one at the local hospital, but this is no ordinary corpse, this is "Bud the Chud," a cannibalistic humanoid underground dweller - out on a killing spree."

My second week into film school, following in the footsteps of Martin Scorsese, I found myself sitting in Freshman Colloquium watching not "Raging Bull", nor "Citizen Kane"... but "C.H.U.D. 2." As if this was not thrilling enough, my classmates and I were treated to a live action commentary on the filmmaking process by the director of the film: the then chair of the Undergraduate Film and TV Department, David Irving.

Mr. Irving is the brother of Amy Irving. And he directed "C.H.U.D 2". Which is apparently all that is required to become the chairman of the Undergraduate Film and TV Department at Tisch School of the Arts at New York University.

During the course of his lecture and commentary, Mr. Irving enlightened us about the process of directing "Bud" in his many shenanigans. It was truly one of the most awe inspiring lectures I have ever attended. What instills me with the most awe, as I reflect back, is that immediately following this screening I did not run to the Bursar's office, demand a complete refund of my first semester's tuition, and drop out of school on the spot.

Save the Faculty

Faculty Support

One of the hallmarks of the Tisch School of the Arts is its faculty of working professional artists – in fact, they one of the reasons the very best and brightest students want to come here. We currently face significant challenges in attracting and retaining the very best faculty members. The cost of living is always a central factor in the life of an artist, and in New York City that cost can be prohibitive. Many people we would like to recruit choose to accept positions elsewhere, where salaries are higher or, at the very least, will stretch farther. In addition, the commitment to students at Tisch is considerable, leaving these individuals little time to develop their own work. Artists should not have to abandon their own artistic endeavors in order to teach. In short, we cannot have distinguished and cutting-edge artists as teachers unless we make it possible for them to continue working on their art.

We seek to raise $20 million for faculty support, which will be used in support of 8 new endowed chairs. $5 million would sustain a "Leave Fund," thus making it possible for faculty members to engage in activities that would enrich their development as artists and scholars through sabbaticals, research, and special projects. The Leave Fund could also support junior faculty members and adjuncts, as well as distinguished visitors.

This blurb is taken directly from Tisch's website, and it sheds a lot of light on why the program is so retarded. The people who teach at Tisch are, by the school's own admission, unable to support themselves financially through their work. They rely on the school to essentially subsidize their artistic endeavors.

How can somebody who has not been able to support themselves through filmmaking possibly teach a young person how to support themselves through filmmaking?

They can't. Which is why the school is so fatally artsy fartsy and impractical. If you look at the resumes of the faculty members, you will see listed among their prestigious accolades a number of grants and fellowships. These are the Oscars of the world of Academia. They carry a kind of intellectual prestige, along with a few bucks, but you can't produce a $10 million movie, or even a $100,000 movie, on a grant. You can't base a film career on having won an award back in 1982, or making obscure documentaries for public television that nobody has ever seen.

Apparently, the only thing that these types of accomplishments *can* do is secure you a tenured, paid position as a film professor.

But the rest of us have to work for a company that is making things that people want to see, or we must make things ourselves that people want to see. Michael Moore and Morgan Spurlock have shown that documentaries can be popular, but their success has more to do with their ability to understand marketing, humor, and muckracking than any intrinsic artistic ability. Brett Ratner, director of "X-Men 2" and "Rush Hour", graduated from NYU Undergrad. He is a success not because of his Fundamentals classes or the tutelage of his professors, but because he knows how to shmooze and work it. He spent more time on music video sets than in his classes during school. He says so himself in the book "Breaking In", by Nick Jarecki.

Promotion, marketing, fundraising, networking, business sense. These are the tools a young person needs when trying to get a film career off the ground. Most students at Tisch are overflowing with artistic talent. That's not where they need help. They need help learning how to mold that talent into a career where they can express themselves as artists *and* enjoy financial success. It's called entrepreneurship. But you won't learn anything about entrepreneurship at Tisch. Instead, you will learn how to be the quintessential "starving artist".

The Administration and the Faculty look at Tisch as an "art" school. They do not recognize that film is an art that is inherently and organically linked with money. Filmmakers do not work in a vacuum. Yet the professors are afforded an environment in which they get to work in a vacuum, with no financial responsibility.

Since the professors do not know what is required to succeed in the business, the students waste the first 2 years of their time and money doing baloney "exercises" with the camera rather than building a reel highlighting their talent and skill which is suitable for the marketplace.

And when each student graduates, he enters an unfriendly and highly competitive marketplace where he is under prepared and deeply in debt, without any real clue about how to land a job or finance his feature project.

And yet, the school is actively seeking Twenty Million Dollars so that Professors can continue to work on their documentaries and experimental art without worrying about rent.

Here's an interesting idea. Why doesn't the school raise Twenty Million Dollars to help fund recent graduates' Feature Film Projects? That could finance 200 films with budgets of $100,000. Or 100 films with $200,000 budgets. Or 50 films with $400,000 budgets. Or 20 films with $1 million budgets.

If the school would help graduates pay for their films, they could be spared much of the drama, heartbreak, and humiliation of typical independent feature film financing. Just imagine a trust fund of millions of dollars for the sole purpose of making the student's filmmaking dreams come true. It would be awe inspiring and heart warming. It would justify the years of time and millions of dollars in loans and tuition the students have invested in the program over the years. It would be something the school could proudly display on their website and present in their news. It would make film school worthwhile.

But I know this is not to be. After all, without an endowment for the professors, we may never see "C.H.U.D. 3".

Chapter 3

Fun With Numbers

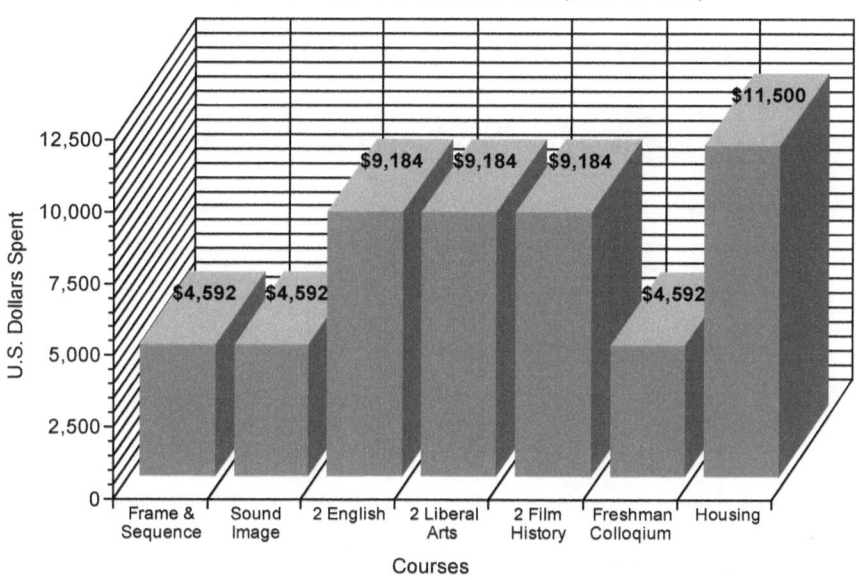

http://www.nyu.edu/financial.aid/tuitiontisch.html

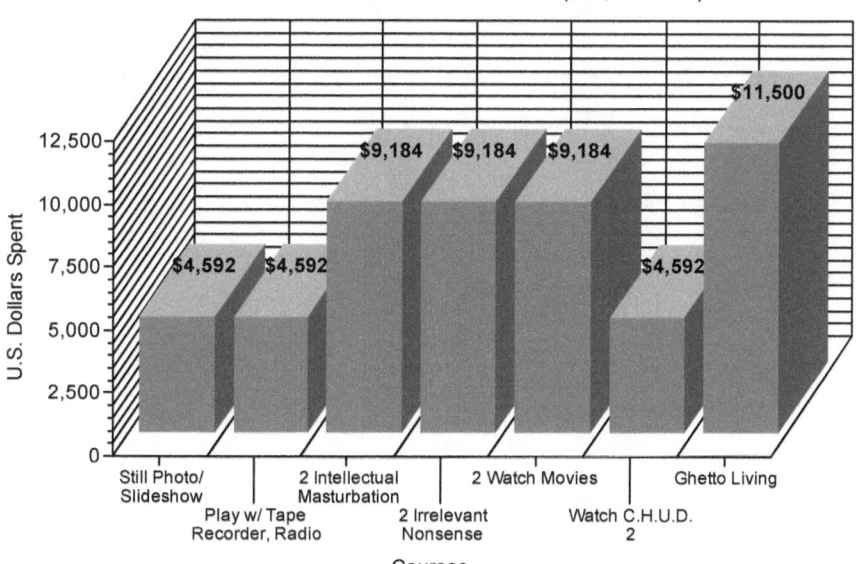

An Actual NYU Film Grad

$52,000 is a lot of money. Theoretically, look at how that money could grow if you left it alone in a well balanced mutual fund.

Time Value Calculator

Time Value Calculator

Your Results

Your investment of **$52,000.00** earning a rate of **7.50%** annually for **40.00** years, would grow to **$1,034,742**, before taxes. This assumes that you do not withdraw investment earnings or make any additional contributions.

This table shows the future value of your investment for different time periods.

Year	Future Value Without Additional Contributions
1	$56,037
2	$60,387
3	$65,075
4	$70,127
5	$75,571
10	$109,827
15	$159,611
20	$231,962
30	$489,920
40	$1,034,742
50	$2,185,442

Please consult a financial advisor about your individual situation. This chart is intended for hypothetical illustration only and is not intended to be representative of past or future performance of any particular investment. This does not take into account costs or fees that may be associated with a particular investment nor do the returns take into consideration the impact of taxes. When investing in securities, the principal and return will fluctuate with changes in market conditions. The above table assumes no fluctuation or loss in principal. Depending on market conditions, you may need to invest more or less than the amounts stated above to help reach your final goal.

Copyright © 2007, Standard & Poor's, a division of The McGraw-Hill Companies, Inc. All rights reserved.

http://fc.standardandpoors.com/htdocs/calculators/atim/calculator.jsp?toolid=000592 8/1/2007 8:54:47 PM

That's your retirement.

You just spent it making a slideshow and a radio drama.

Whack!

Question: what was that sound?

Answer: Your 65 year old self teleporting back in time and slapping you upside the head.

Heck, it doesn't even have to be your 65 year old self slapping you upside the head. It could be your future self who has just graduated film school. Or who has just finished this book. Or even this chapter. I'm here, look at what you could buy with just a portion of that $52,000 after choosing to skip film school:

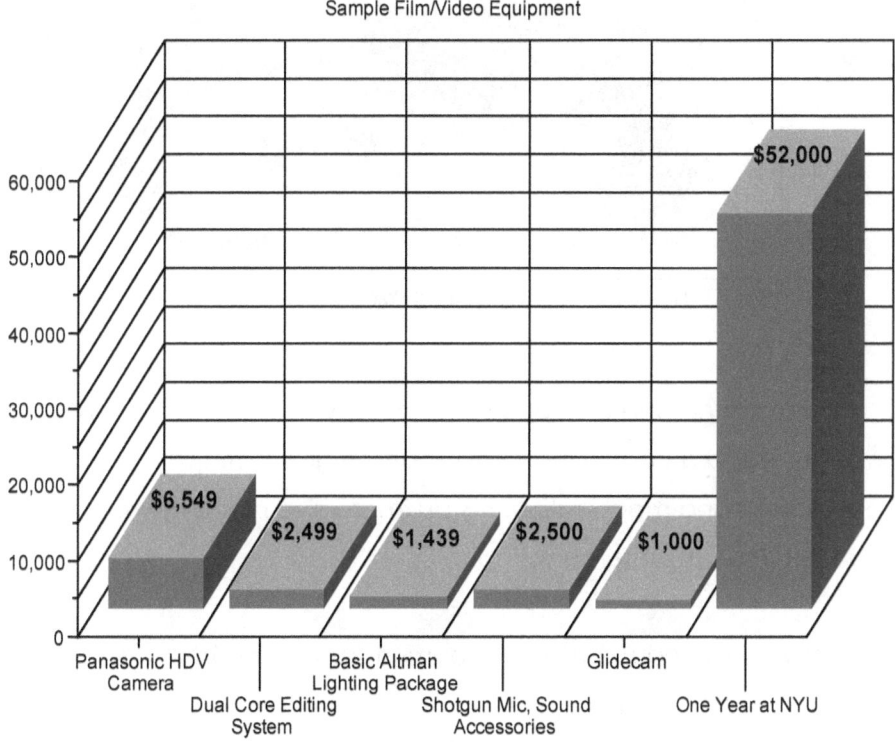

I have to fess up: I really enjoy illustrating my points with bar graphs. In fact, if I were to try and illustrate how much I enjoy illustrating points with bar graphs, using a bar graph, it might look like this:

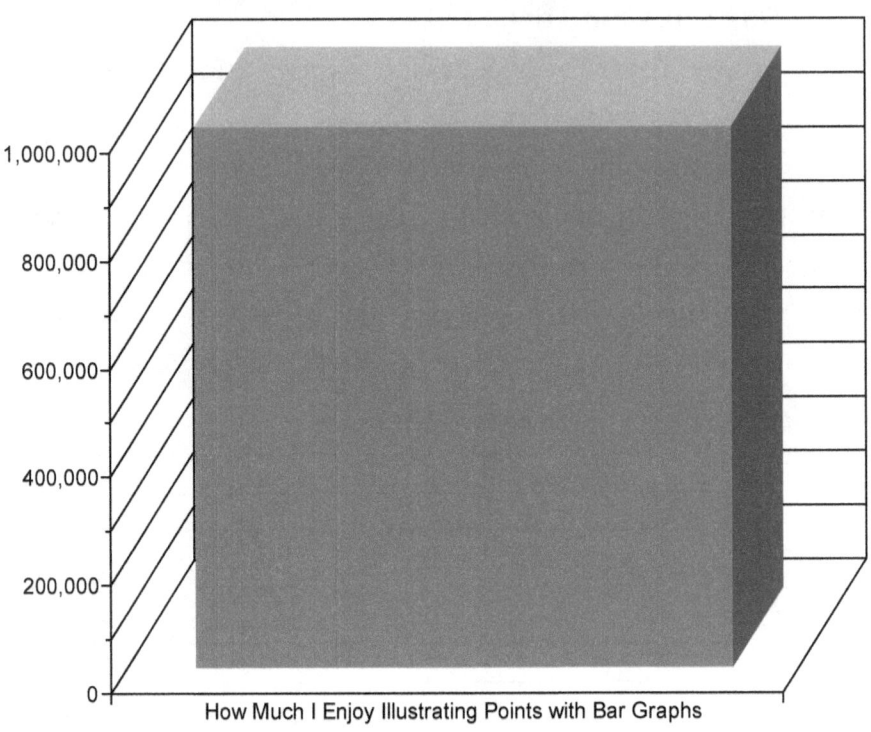

But I'm not the only one with an affinity for Bar Graphs. NYU has compiled a comprehensive report on graduate job placement and mean salary. It's an impressive piece of work. You can find it on the internet at:

http://www.nyu.edu/careerdevelopment/survey/2006/fulltime.php

And it features a number of stunning bar graphs. Like this one:

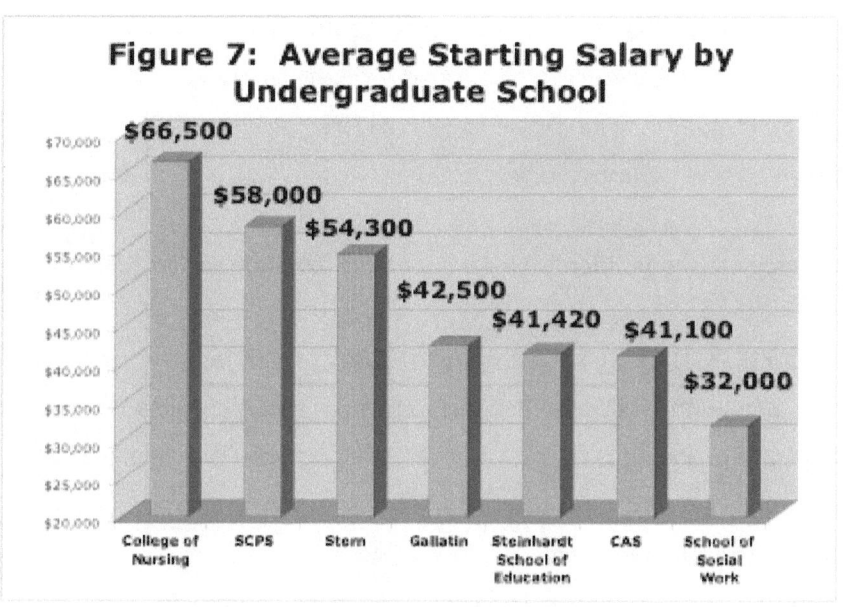

But wait, hold on a second.

Where's Tisch? It isn't even on this beautiful bar graph.

That's because Tisch was not, nor has it ever been, held accountable for job placement statistics. It's probably a good thing, too, because it would really "lower the bar", so to speak.

You will be *lucky* to make $30,000 annually ($15 an hour) your first year out of school. You'll average less real money because in this field, you work much more than 8 hours a day. Plus, crew work is irregular. And the other jobs pay as about as well if you were a migrant worker. But unlike a migrant worker, you have to pay taxes. In spite of all this, I'll say the average starting salary for a film grad is $33,000, because the idea that a filmmaker would make less than a Social Worker is just sad. By the way, if you've never had to work full time, you should know that $33,000 a year comes down to about $500 a week after taxes.

Since Tisch doesn't keep any financial stats on its grads, I had to look at NYU as a whole. According to the Project on Student Debt, in 2005 the average NYU grad walked away with $29,480 in debt. By 2006, this figure rose to $34, 417. Check out their extensive, non partisan report at:

http://projectonstudentdebt.org/files/pub/State_by_State_report_FINAL.pdf

But $34,417 is just the average. Sure, it means some people walk away with less debt. But it also means some people walk away with more. Lots more. I've heard of people graduating with as much as $70,000 and up in student loans. That's a mighty blow to your monthly expenses.

But don't worry. The Student Loan companies want to work with you. They aren't going to make you pay up all at once. Instead, they let you pay it back over 10 or 20 years, for a slight charge. It's called *interest*. Remember in the chart a few pages ago, where the $52,000 spent on freshman year invested in a mutual fund eventually *earns* you a million dollars over 40 years? Well, in this scenario, you have a chance to give back to the wonderful corporate conglomerate or government entity that has made your higher education possible. This time, instead of getting paid by the market, you pay them 7 percent or so on the money you've borrowed. Doesn't seem like it could be that much, right? Well, let's take a trip over to www.finaid.org:

The SmartStudent Guide to Financial Aid

Site Map   About FinAid

- Loans
- Scholarships
- Savings
- Military Aid

Other Types of Aid

Financial Aid Applications

Answering Your Questions

Calculators

Beyond Financial Aid

[SEARCH]

Loan Calculator

Loan Balance:	$34,417.00
Adjusted Loan Balance:	$34,417.00
Loan Interest Rate:	6.80%
Loan Fees:	0.00%
Loan Term:	10 years
Minimum Payment:	$50.00
Monthly Loan Payment:	**$396.07**
Number of Payments:	120
Cumulative Payments:	$47,528.74
Total Interest Paid:	$13,111.74

Note: The monthly loan payment was calculated at 119 payments of $396.07 plus a final payment of $396.41.

It is estimated that you will need an annual salary of at least $47,528.40 to be able to afford to repay this loan. This estimate assumes that 10% of your gross monthly income will be devoted to repaying your student loans. If you use 15% of your gross monthly income to repay the loan, you will need an annual salary of only $31,685.60, but you may experience some financial difficulty.

See, isn't that easy? It will only cost you an additional $13,111.74 dollars in interest to pay this loan off in 10 years. (Almost as much as 3 profound English classes!) No sweat.

But wait. It's estimated that you'll need to be making at least $47,528.40 a year to afford to pay back the loan comfortably. After all, $391.06 a month could lease you a Lexus. That's quite a hefty sum when you consider rent, health insurance, clothes, food, transportation... all those things you never thought about when you were in school because... well, everything was being paid for by the student loans.

But don't worry! You can pay the loan off in 15 years and it will cost you less each month. Thank God. Let's see what that looks like:

Loan Calculator

Loan Balance:	$34,417.00
Adjusted Loan Balance:	$34,417.00
Loan Interest Rate:	6.80%
Loan Fees:	0.00%
Loan Term:	15 years
Minimum Payment:	$50.00
Monthly Loan Payment:	**$305.51**
Number of Payments:	181
Cumulative Payments:	$54,993.11
Total Interest Paid:	$20,576.11

- Loans
- Scholarships
- Savings
- Military Aid
- Other Types of Aid
- Financial Aid Applications
- Answering Your Questions
- Calculators
- Beyond Financial Aid

Note: The monthly loan payment was calculated at 180 payments of $305.51 plus a final payment of $1.31.

It is estimated that you will need an annual salary of at least $36,661.20 to be able to afford to repay this loan. This estimate assumes that 10% of your gross monthly income will be devoted to repaying your student loans. If you use 15% of your gross monthly income to repay the loan, you will need an annual salary of only $24,440.80, but you may experience some financial difficulty.

Okay, so now it's only $305.51 a month or so. That saves you $85.55 a month. Much more manageable. And it's estimated you will only need to be making about $36,661.20 a year (which you won't be making) to pay it off comfortably. And all it costs you in the long run is another $7,464.37 in interest and 5 more years of monthly payments. Okay. So now your $34,417 loan has cost you a total of $54,993.11. (More than a full year's tuition and housing!)

Well, that's not so bad. It's better than what happens when you need 20 years to pay off the loan. That lowers your monthly payment to $262.72, which is $42.79 a month less than the 10 year loan. That may not be much, but if you aren't lucky enough to be making $30,000 and have to work one of the many $9-$14 an hour jobs in the biz, you may need that extra cash each month.

The SmartStudent Guide to Financial Aid

Site Map About FinAid

- Loans
- Scholarships
- Savings
- Military Aid

Other Types of Aid

Financial Aid Applications

Answering Your Questions

Calculators

Beyond Financial Aid

Loan Calculator

Loan Balance:	$34,417.00
Adjusted Loan Balance:	$34,417.00
Loan Interest Rate:	6.80%
Loan Fees:	0.00%
Loan Term:	20 years
Minimum Payment:	$50.00
Monthly Loan Payment:	**$262.72**
Number of Payments:	240
Cumulative Payments:	$63,052.07
Total Interest Paid:	$28,635.07

Note: The monthly loan payment was calculated at 239 payments of $262.72 plus a final payment of $261.99.

It is estimated that you will need an annual salary of at least $31,526.40 to be able to afford to repay this loan. This estimate assumes that 10% of your gross monthly income will be devoted to repaying your student loans. If you use 15% of your gross monthly income to repay the loan, you will need an annual salary of only $21,017.60, but you may experience some financial difficulty.

All it will cost you is another $8,058. Only eight thousand dollars to save $43 a month. That means your total interest paid is $28,635. Almost the full amount of the original loan. And the total you've paid over those twenty years is $63,052.

SIXTY THREE THOUSAND DOLLARS.

That means you're 38 years old and instead of having a nice chunk of money in the bank, working *for* you, you've been paying Wachovia or the Federal Government tons of money every year so you could listen to the wisdom of a Cable Ace Award Winner.

Another Way

Imagine you've been saving for your child's education since birth. You put $200 away every month, about the same cost as the eventual student loan. By the time he's 18, you've got more than

$40,000 saved. The school is happy to take that lump sum, your child earns some scholarships and grants, and takes out $30,000 in loans. He ends up with a debt equal to or greater than his annual salary.

Now, imagine that instead of spending the $40,000 you've been saving, the kid skips skip college and goes right to work in the biz. Even though he's making very little, he manages to save $200 a month… less than the cost of a student loan payment. He adds this to his savings. Even if the family had saved nothing for college, he still has almost $10,000 saved up. And eventually, he will start earning more money.

By age 22, you've got some very different scenarios:

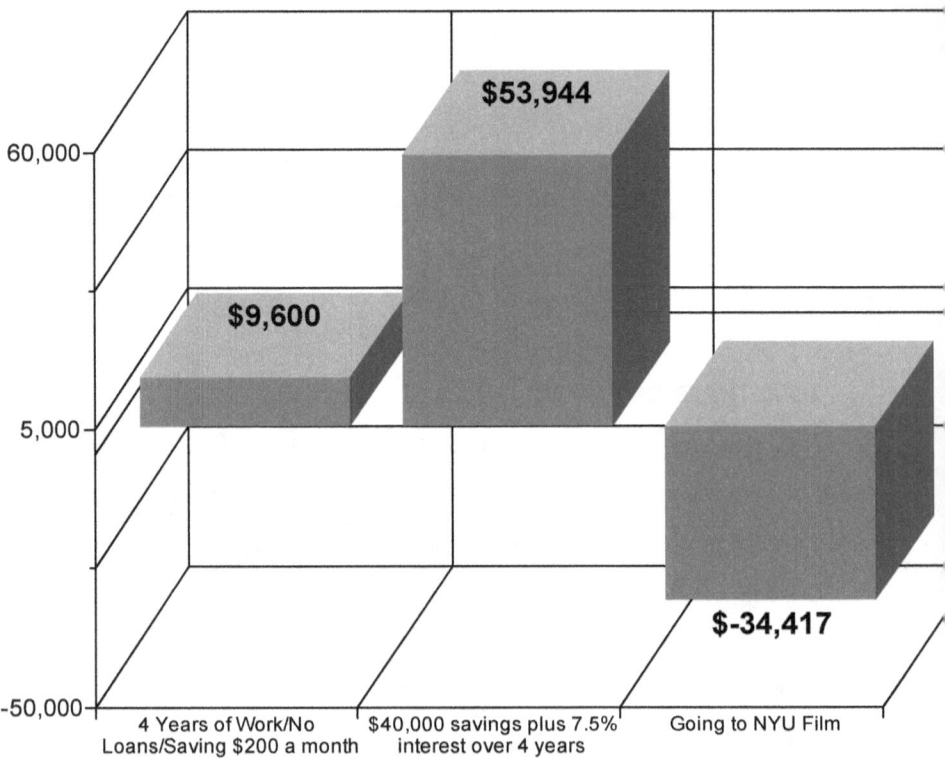

Now, I know I've only gotten as far as Freshman Year. Typically, a discussion about finances, loans, and debt comes at the end on school.

But that's stupid. Unfortunately, its how most of us have been taught to approach college. We're taught to focus on getting in, getting approval from the professors, borrowing money, earning scholarships, and graduating. And then, like waking up for a 4 year bender, we get hit with the tab and hope for the best. But college costs a lot more than a night of binge drinking. And it can produce a financial headache that won't go away with a glass of orange juice and some aspirin.

Part 2: The Sophomore Year

So, you've finally mastered the inner workings of a tape recorder and a still camera. You've made a slideshow and identified random sounds of the city. You've blown $12,000 to take an English class and watch old movies. And now, you are finally ready to work with film and video.

But wait! Slow down there, NYU! Short films, which we could put on our reel, enter into film festivals and show to potential investors, studio executives, or producers? Color film and video, with complete storylines and dialogue after only one full year of school? You've got to be crazy!

Well fear not, fair student, we wouldn't want you be overwhelmed. Instead of burdening you with the possibility of making cohesive narratives with dialogue, and confusing you with colors like blue and orange, we're going to gently ease your transition into the world of moving pictures by letting you play with silent, black and white film cameras. And make documentaries. Even if you don't want to make documentaries. And direct a sitcom.

Chapter 4

The Silent Revolution

Fundamentals of Sight & Sound: Film

H56.0043   Studio   6 Credits

Course Level: Fundamental

Course is <u>not</u> repeatable.
Prerequisite: Sophomore status.

Students should not schedule any other course on the same days as Sight & Sound.

All students taking Fundamentals of Sight & Sound: Film must register for the corresponding (i.e., the same section number) of Tech Theory: Film, H56.1030, for 1 point.

Sophomore-level students are required to take the following course as a prerequisite for any upper-level film production courses. Groups of four students each join together to produce short B&W reversal non-sync films. Each student will write and direct five films and rotate in crew positions. The first three projects are silent; the fourth incorporates either sound effects, narration or music; the fifth allows the student to use multiple tracks. Students follow specific exercises with technical guidelines but are encouraged to express themselves creatively. The emphasis centers on elements of storytelling through a broad spectrum of aesthetic approaches. Students are introduced to working in collaboration with fellow students while maintaining individual means of expression. Student work is screened and critiqued by both faculty and class. During the first week of class students will be advised about purchasing a required light meter.

If you ever find yourself watching a black and white film with no sound you can be assured that you are watching either:

1. A movie made pre-1918, before the advent of "talkies"
2. A very obscure "art house" film
3. A screening of "Charlie's Angels" gone horribly, horribly wrong
4. A student film

Film school provides students with a unique opportunity to work with outdated and discontinued film equipment they would otherwise be completely unaware of. Allow me to elaborate.

If you've ever shot a home video and played it on your TV, you know that you get both picture *and* sound at the same time. That's because a video tape has tracks for both video and audio. But film works differently.

All film cameras, even the ones used in Hollywood movies, just record picture. Sound is recorded separately, usually on a digital audio tape (DAT). But in order for the sounds and dialogue you are recording to play back normally, the film camera and the digital audio tape have to be "in synch". This is to say, they need to be recorded at the same speed. Otherwise, your movie will look like a poorly dubbed Japanese anime, which people's mouths moving way out of synch with the dialogue.

So all modern film cameras are called "synch" cameras. They have a little crystal chip inside of them that makes sure they run at a constant speed which will match up exactly with the speed of the sound being recorded.

Before the advent of synch cameras, most film cameras were "non synch". Which means that their speed fluctuates ever so slightly while you are filming. And if you try and record dialogue to match the picture, people's mouths are going to start moving all out of synch with the words.

Nobody uses these cameras anymore

Except for film students.

And nobody makes these cameras anymore.

So the school is still using the same cameras it bought back in the 60s.

ARRIFLEX S  Package consists of 1 Camera body w/variable speed motor 1 Cine 60 Battery Belt w/built in charger 3 Zeiss Prime lenses (8mm, 25mm, 50mm)	$150.00 Day rate

Source: http://www.hitandrunproductions.com/16mm.htm

The cameras are old, batted, beaten, and weathered. They have to be. They've been used by thousands of film students for more than 30 years. But the cameras can't be as old as the Steenbeck Flatbed Editing machines which we used to edit our films.

ROOM 1171: SIGHT AND SOUND FILM/STEENBECK FLATBEDS

This lab is available for any student currently enrolled in Sight and Sound Film. Students have access to the Steenbecks in 3 ways: lab time, walk-ins, and reservations made through the class TA. Sight and Sound Film uses 6 plate steenbecks.

Equipment:
- (21) Sight and Sound Film Steenbecks
- Rewind tables

Classes Handled: Sight and Sound Film

A 20 YEAR OLD PAYING $8,036 TO USE OBSOLETE EQUIPMENT.

Flatbed editing consists of actually threading spools of film stock through a small view finder. When you see the part you want to edit, you have to mark the film with an "x" using a magic marker. Then you cut the film with a razor blade. You find the next point on the film you wish to "cut" to, mark it with a marker, cut it with a razor blade, and you literally tape the two pieces of film together with a piece of scotch tape.

Flatbed Editing was the industry standard for many, many years. Then, in the 1990s, people began editing using a new technology called "computers". Now, the time consuming process of marking film, physically cutting and splicing it with razor blades and tape, can be accomplished with the click of a button.

Computer editing has become so common that every single Macintosh computer sold today comes bundled with "iMovie", a basic computer editing software program. Young children with only basic motor skills are editing their own movies with bright colors and happy music.

But not NYU Film students.

It is difficult to determine exactly what aspect of this course adequately reflects exactly how stupid the Administration thinks that you are. It could be:

1. Charging you $8,036 (6 credits at $1,148 a credit, plus another 1 credit for Tech Theory) to use ancient film cameras that rent for $150 a day (and where you will have about 6 shooting days total)
2. Requiring you to edit your films on a completely obsolete technology (with scotch tape, nonetheless.)
3. Requiring you to take a course of this nature before allowing you to even consider creating a coherent, presentable narrative, with sound and color
4. Continuing to present themselves as one of the leading film schools in the country after wasting another semester of

your time and money on something so impractical and wasteful

My Professor for this course had long, beautiful hair. He would toss his head back periodically to let it breathe. He enjoyed using the word "exquisite" to describe things he liked very much. When using the word "exquisite" he would hold out one hand dramatically, with the index finer touching his thumb. He gave our class detailed feedback on our work, like "you might want to lose that shot" and "well, if you were going for cheesy, you nailed it."

I can hardly fault him. With classes of 30 and up, it is almost impossible for a Professor to spent adequate time with each student. But I really did miss out. After all, this Professor did collaborate as co-author on 6 Lucy Kaplansky albums.

Calling the people who teach these classes "Professor" is a little like calling the guy who turns on the music system at Applebee's "Maestro". The actual caliber of educational exchange going on is virtually nil. The basic elements of filmmaking are covered in a few required textbooks like "Shot by Shot." That is, by the way, a great book. It talks about wide shots, editing, shot composition, narrative... all of the important things your film "Professor" won't have time to get into. Because he'll be too busy showing you scenes from "The Godfather" and telling you how exquisite they are.

The "Professor's" actual feedback truly is limited to a few comments after the screening of the film. You get to evaluate your own learning experience in a report you hand in for each film you make. The Prof gives you a letter grade along with some wise words like "Good job". (I'm serious). You write the film, shoot it, cut it, screen it, write your own review of it and then, if you go on to become famous, the school will say that the reason you were so successful is because of their AMAZING instruction!

Vaseline

One of the little morsels of information we gleaned from "Sight and Sound: Film" was that back in the old days, filmmakers put Vaseline over the lenses of their cameras in order to give the image that soft, "Soap Opera" look. As usual it was great trivia, albeit completely useless with today's modern film equipment.

But since we were using archaic black and white cameras, we could mount them with a clear slate of glass and smear Vaseline on them, just like in the 1950s.

One night I was hanging out with my roomies and the girls next door. Our dorm consisted of two rooms. We mostly watched TV and drank in the outer room. My friend Ross and I were lucky enough to inhabit the more private inner room.

Ross and I had to get up early the next day for film class, so we excused ourselves and asked our buddies to keep it down. As I lay in bed, I was still coming up with ideas for my next film. I was seriously considering doing a Soap Opera, and I wanted to try that little lens gimmick. But I didn't have the proper tools.

So I hopped out of bed and walked into the main room, still wearing my boxers. Everyone stopped and looked at me.

"Hey," I said, rubbing my eyes, "does anybody have any Vaseline?"

They looked at me, their mouths agape.

Suppressing a laugh, Jen finally said, "Um… sorry Seth."

"Thanks anyway," I said with disappointment, then stumbled back into my room.

As I closed the door, I heard everyone burst into raucous laughter.

Ross sat up in bed.

"What happened? Did you say something funny?

"No," I said, confused. "I just went out there and asked if they had any Vaseline."

Ross looked at me with alarm.

"Dude," he said slowly, "why do you need Vaseline?"

"You know, for the lens. The camera lens. To make a Soap Opera."

Ross look relieved, but he shook his head and laughed.

"What?!" I said, still confused.

"Dude... we just went to bed. You walk out there in your boxers... ask for Vaseline..."

"So?"

Ross put his hand over his head.

"Dude, they think....!"

It slowly dawned on me.

"Oh shit," I said and ran outside.

Everyone was still laughing.

"It's for a film project!" I yelled. "We are not butt fucking!"

It took me a long time to live that one down.

My Affinity for Tin Cans

Sadly, I did not learn the basics of how to tell a visual story from my film school. I learned them from Mr. Tschorke in my 11th grade Video Communications class. He taught us about cutting on action, framing, and the 180 degree rule. I practiced with a VHS camcorder and, by copying my favorite movies, learned how to frame people so they looked like they were having a conversation and how to create an action sequence. I showed my friends how to do the same thing. It's easy!

At the time I was taking "Sight and Sound: Film", I didn't care. I love making movies. I put up with the teacher's insipid lectures and inane comments and the fact that I was unable to record funny dialogue because at least I was filming something, a refreshing change from the bizarre Freshman year. I also had a bunch of great friends and I was in New York City. I had a good time. It was fun. I was distracted.

It wasn't until years later that I realized I'd been had.

After all, in 1994, I took a basic 16mm filmmaking class at the Visual Studies Workshop (www.vsw.org) in Rochester, NY. For $300, I learned how to write, shoot, and edit a short 16mm film. I was still in high school.

I forgot I already had this skill, because I assumed that by my Sophomore year I would be making color films with sound. And that's why I came here in the first place, right? But sadly, I hadn't made a real movie of any kind since the VHS videos I'd shot in high school a year and half before. I was still learning the "Fundamentals".

Which is still perplexing to me.

After all, if the school is truly a destination for the best and brightest, why do they waste TWO YEARS on "Fundamentals" when in other programs you can pick up a camera on day one? Are they implying that their students are RETARDED?

I don't think so. I have to give the school some credit. I just learned that finally, in Fall of 2007, the school will begin phasing out the Steenbeck Flatbed Editing Machines. The reason? According to a current film student, NYU can no longer find ANYBODY IN THE WORLD to service these machines. It's like trying to find an 8 Track repairman.

Finally, Sight and Sound students will be able to learn computer editing software to edit their narratives, just like your neighbor's kids down the street.

Now I know it may seem like I've been a bit harsh on the school and their curriculum. After all, it was a great experience to actually touch the film, see all the frames, and cut it with my bare hands. But it was kind of like going to the science museum, learning how the first telephone was created, and making a phone out of two tin cans and a piece of string. It's a fun, tactile, interactive exercise that gives you a greater appreciation for the roots of the technology.

But when you leave the museum, do you call your girlfriend on a tin can? If so, you probably don't have a girlfriend. And you have an alarming affinity for tin cans.

Computer editing technology has been available since the late nineties. It is now the industry standard. It should be taught from day one.

But that would be too practical. After all, this is a prestigious Academic Institution.

Chapter 5

Sitcoms & Documentaries

Fundamentals of Sight & Sound: Television

H56.0050   Studio   6 Credits

Course Level: Fundamental *(formerly Sight&Sound Video)* Please note: *This course is no longer offered. It has been split into Sight and Sound: Studio (H56.0051) and Sight and Sound: Documentary (H56.0080)*

Prerequisite: Sophomore status. **Sophomore-level students are required to take the following course as a prerequisite for any upper-level video/television production course.**

Sight and Sound : Television is an introductory course in Television Production. Students shoot three multiple-camera, live-to-tape, narrative studio projects and two single-camera, on-location, documentary projects. Working on a rotation basis in the TV12 Studios, students learn to operate all studio production equipment as they write, direct, produce and crew for each other. Working in crews of four in the field, students learn location sound, lighting, and all aspects of field production. They also receive complete training in Avid post-production editing. Through this series of five short projects (three studio, two documentary) the course introduces students to the collaborative process while demanding the expression of an individual voice. All student work is screened and critiqued by faculty and fellow classmates.

Students should not schedule any other course on the same days as Sight & Sound. All students taking Fundamentals of Sight & Sound: Studio must register for the corresponding (i.e., the same section number) of Tech Theory: Studio, H56.1029, for 1 point.

Recent television production has proven that the medium has incredible possibilities never previously imagined. Shows like "Lost", "24", "6 Feet Under", and "The Sopranos" have thrilled viewers with their rich characterizations and complex storylines. These critically acclaimed shows have illustrated that TV can actually surpass film in terms of creating deep, fully developed fictional universes for audiences to become lost in.

It should then come as no surprise that NYU's approach to the world of television is dated, remedial, and takes advantage of none of these advances in the medium. Instead, you are required to either engage in basic video exercises or learn how to direct a sitcom.

You have a choice between two courses: "Sight and Sound: Studio" or "Sight and Sound: Documentary." It's kind of like having to choose between dirt or booger flavored ice cream.

"Sight and Sound: Studio" takes place in the ancient realm of the Tisch 12th Floor Television Studios, built many, many years ago. The equipment is as old as the mentality behind the course. For a mere 6 credits ($6,888) you will create 4 studio projects. The technical theory component of the course, where they actually teach you how to use the TV cameras and switchers and lights, is another credit ($1,148). And since this requires you to (finally) work with actors and dialogue, they add in another 2 credits and call this aspect of the course "Acting for the Camera I". And that only costs you another $2,296. So, all in all, the course is 9 credits and costs $10,332.

"Sight and Sound: Documentary" is your first opportunity to work with a new, cutting edge technology called a "video camera". As a Tisch student, you may have never actually heard of these tiny wonders. They are small electronic devices that can record high quality picture *and* sound onto a small "mini-DV" video tape. The course is 6 credits plus tech theory for another credit, so it costs a little less than "Sight and Sound: Studio". It's only $8,036.

Now I know what you're thinking. You're thinking, "But Seth, I have no interest in documentary. I own my own non linear editing system on a Mac, so why should I pay to use the school's? I also have no interest in studio production. I want to work on feature films or episodic TV! I want to learn about creating a season long story arch and character development, and how to shoot on location with cranes and how to storyboard and manage a crew! Or at least how to get a job as a Writer's Assistant. And why does it cost between $8,000 and $10,000?!"

Shhhh. Shhh... quiet down, little college student. The people at NYU Film are professionals. They've been doing this for 30 years, and people continue to believe that their program is top notch. So it must be. Besides, you need this course to go on and finally make a *real* film!

"Well, okay. I guess."

Now that you've been duped into taking one of these stupid courses, let's see what this semester has in store.

Sight and Sound: Studio

"Sight and Sound: Studio", the booger flavored ice cream, gives you the opportunity to create 4 projects in the studio. The first project requires you to use still pictures put to music. That's right, even though the studio features 3 cameras, you will only be using one. And it's going to be locked into position, shooting a *still fucking photo* you took with a *still fucking camera* outside of the studio. And you're going to make a slideshow, and put it to music. And I'm not kidding. What is with this school and slideshows?

Okay, well at least once that is out of the way, you can *finally* direct a scene working with real live actors and dialogue. Write a scene... oh wait, hold on. When I attended the school back in 1996, we were allowed to write and create our own sketches. But now, you have to choose from a number of scripts that have already been written. These are usually scenes from movies with the names of the characters removed so you can't readily place where they came from. A recent grad of the course told me his scenes came from "Proof" and a friend's came from "Hannah and Her Sisters."

Now, it should be noted that TV dramas are no longer shot in 3 camera studios. That stopped a long time ago. The film scripts you are assigned came from stories shot on film with one camera on location, with no switcher or studio equipment. The kind of camera used to shoot "Proof" or "Hannah and Her Sisters" is completely different from the TV Cameras you use in the studio. It's a completely different experience. In fact, TV Studio cameras are only used to shoot things like "According to Jim", the nightly news, or Oprah.

So the possibility of you finding yourself directing a dramatic scene in a 3 camera studio environment in the professional world of TV is about as likely as finding yourself editing a movie on one of those outdated Steenbeck Flatbed Editing machines. It simply doesn't make any sense.

At least you finally get a chance to try your hand at some "directing". But it does bring to mind one question. If all of the "Fundamental" courses are supposed to be building upon each other, then what course has been preparing you to finally direct actors? Was it the slideshow class? Or was it the one with the tape recorder, or the silent movies?

Truth is, you've never really worked with actors before. And now you're just going to have to learn to direct actors by... going ahead and directing them! The classes you took previous to this were completely irrelevant.

Okay, that's fine. You are finally directing. But wait... the Studio course is 6 credits. That's 6 credits to make 4 projects. Fine. But then what's with the extra 2 credits for "Acting for the Camera?" Isn't that part of the course already? I mean, you're supposed to be making pieces that feature actors in scenes. Shouldn't the professor giving you guidance on directing actors be part of the 6 credit course?

Or, if you are going to take a class on "Acting for the Camera" for 2 credits, shouldn't it be taught separately? After all, you only go to class 2 days a week, from 9 AM to 5:30 PM. The "Sight and Sound: Documentary" course meets during the same time, but it's only 6 credits plus tech theory.

And, according to a current Tisch student, once you've actually shot your project, most of the class time is spent watching people's projects. That takes days and days of class. Which means the actual amount of time you are in the studio, working with the actors, or receiving instruction on how to direct actors for the camera, is extremely limited.

Now let's delve even deeper into this "Acting for the Camera" bullshit. It's a bullshit title for a bullshit course that doesn't even really exist. It's just something the Administration tacked on to an already worthless class. Chances are that your Professor doesn't know dick about directing actors for the camera. And even if he does, he isn't going to have the time or the ability to give you two credits ($2,296) worth of instruction on the subject. Besides, since you are probably going to have only one day of shooting time for each project, how much instruction could you receive? All of the real work you will do with your actors will be in rehearsals, on your own time, away from class.

This is part of Tisch's brilliance. They let the students do all of the work, and then if you make something great, they will take the credit.

Now, for the 3rd and 4th Studio projects. You've finally shot a scene with two actors. Why not introduce a *third?* That's your 3rd studio project. Directing a pre-written script with 3 characters. Then, for your final project, you are given the opportunity to write your own scene and shoot it, pending the brilliant Professor's approval.

Sight and Sound: Documentary

The school has a very loose interpretation of the term "Documentary". I recall that my first documentary assignment was to "document a person *engaged in an action*". Whoa! I get to video tape somebody *doing something!*

This was an amazing opportunity for me to really delve into the many facets of my own personal, artistic expression. Gee. I could video tape somebody... riding a bike! Or baking a cake! Or eating a watermelon! Or blowing $8,000 on a retarded, mandatory video course!

I've checked in with current students at Tisch. The fundamental curriculum for this course is, of course, pretty much the same as it was back in the late 90s. Except now, you're given 5 assignments. Essentially, each assignment is to make a little documentary on something, and they get progressively longer as the semester goes on.

I've heard different versions of some of the guidelines students are given. In one class, the new first assignment is a little more specific. Instead of recording someone engaged in an action, you are to work with a member of your crew, and interview him or her about his hopes and dreams. These dreams may include someday actually making a film with color and sound.

The formula for Coke has been a trade secret for the last hundred years. Karrass, Ltd. charges corporate clients like Microsoft and Lockheed Martin thousands of dollars to conduct seminars on Effective Negotiating. Stephen King is paid millions for his best selling novels.

What do these three things have in common? They are all intellectual property. Valuable intellectual property. Selling this property for profit, if you are not the owner, is a breach of law.

Because NYU charges students $8,000 to tell them to "video tape your fellow crew member's goals", then "make a little documentary", it's kind of like I just gave away the school's intellectual property.

There's only one difference. The intellectual property owned by Coke, Karrass, and King actually provides something of value to its clients. Coke provides a refreshing and tasty beverage. Karrass gives companies the skills they need to excel in business negotiations. And Stephen King instills people with horror.

NYU Film also instills people with horror. But only when you've realized that the intellectual property you are paying so dearly for is no more valuable than something you could have found in a book at Barnes and Noble.

I'm not kidding.

You are given your camera, some basic instructions, and the rest is up to you. It is no different than if you were to just pick up a camera by yourself and begin experimenting. Except if you did that, you would have the freedom to create whatever you wanted. You could have been doing so for the past 2 years instead of completing vapid "exercises" thought up by the morons of Academia. But instead, you're paying $8,000 to videotape your buddy eating Cheetos.

The Most Expensive Tinkle You've Ever Taken

I recently paid a visit to Glendale Community College here in Los Angeles. Their facilities are not as sprawling or expansive as NYU's, and the real estate is certainly cheaper. But their video cameras and TV Studios are pretty much on a par with what is offered at what is still considered to be one of the best Film Schools in the country.

They have Panasonic DVX-100 video cameras, which are superior to the Sony PD-150 cameras currently used in "Sight and Sound: Documentary". And they have a 3 camera TV Studio like the ones on the 12th floor at Tisch. Anyone can sign up for a class. Once receiving some basic instruction in operation and craft (how to light a scene and operate a studio camera) you are pretty much allowed to create whatever you want. The studio is yours. Or you can take one of their digital cameras out on location and use their computer editing equipment.

And the cost?

$20 A CREDIT.
EACH CLASS IS THREE CREDITS.
SO EACH CLASS COSTS $60.
SIXTY DOLLARS.

If you're enrolled in a class at NYU, try this. Get up during a lecture and go take a leak. Congratulations. You've just spent $60.

Okay, I am exaggerating a little bit. But it did start me wondering just how much you are paying for each minute of time at the school. So, I broke it down. Unfortunately, I was unable to incorporate any bar graphs. On the plus side, I did get to do some math.

Alright, now these calculations are not exact, but they are pretty close. Each semester at NYU runs about 14 weeks or so. "Sight and Sound" classes meet 2 times a week from 9 to 5:30. With lunch, that's about 8 hours per class, twice a week, for 16 hours a week. Times 14 weeks is 224 hours of class. As we all recall, the cost is $8,036 for "Sight and Sound: Documentary" and $10,332 for "Sight and Sound: Studio".

That means that, technically, every hour of "Sight and Sound: Documentary" costs you $35.88. And every hour of "Sight and Sound: Studio" costs you $46.12 an hour. Just for fun, imagine how much your annual salary would be if you made $46.12 an hour. That's just shy of $100,000 a year. Only $70,000 more than you can expect to make upon graduation!

But I really should amend my previous statement. Going to the john during "Sight and Sound: Studio" won't cost you $60. That is, unless you are experiencing some kind of terrible gastrointestinal trauma, resulting in an hour and a half bowel movement. That would cost you $60. Or, the same cost as a semester of equipment and studio access at Glendale Community college. You can reflect on this as you wipe.

The morning of your "Sight and Sound" class will usually be a lecture. This is the case with film, documentary, or studio. Make sure you pay close attention. You never know what jewels of wisdom will be imparted over the course of the next 3 hours. After all, your professor did win the James L. Hearst Guest Lecturer

Award in the Arts and Humanities at the University of Northern Iowa.

Then, after you have received thorough and detailed instruction on how to push the "on" button on the camera and load a tape, you will spend the afternoons of your course out in the field. Sometimes.

Sadly, during my "Sight and Sound: Video" class, I once found myself dozing during a lecture. I looked over at my buddy Mitch. He was doodling in his notebook. A couple of girls in back of the classroom were quietly gossiping and giggling. Another kid had a handheld video game.

It was like being back in high school. At $46 an hour.

Looking back, I am so saddened. My Professor had a PhD from Harvard and had directed tapes for the Port Authority of New Jersey. We could have learned so much from sitting there and listening to her go on and on and on and on and on.

But alas, we were too weak. We became distracted.

Having missed the value of the lecture, we would then venture out into the world with our cameras, completely uncertain about what to do. If only we had paid attention.

How is a young person supposed to know how to make a movie without listening to 20 or more hours of lecture?

"How?!" I ask you, "HOW?!"

Just look at the films of Alfred Hitchcock and Quentin Tarantino. They are so awful. Uninventive. Unintelligent. Boring. Unpopular. If only they had had a chance to sit in a classroom and listen to lectures for hours on end, perhaps they would have produced something of merit.

Part 3: The Junior and Senior Years

Okay. You've finally shot some silent black and white films on ancient film cameras. You've used "video cameras" to create searing documentaries about your classmate's hopes and dreams. You've even begun to learn how to edit using a "computer".

You've sunk $100,000 and 2 years into this program.

And now, it is time.

It is finally time for you to realize your dream.

You are finally going to have a chance... to do some acting.

Chapter 6
Method Spending

Actor's Craft I

H56.1024   Studio   3 Credits

Course Level: Fundamental

Course is repeatable; you may take up to 9 points total of Actor's Craft I and Actor's Craft II.

Intended for film and television directors, the course is a practical exploration of basic elements of the actor's craft: different methods of approach to script material, terminology, and the working relationship of the actor with the director.

Attending NYU Film gives you the rare opportunity to pay Three Thousand Dollars for an Acting Class.

The 54 Credits of Film Related courses required for graduating cannot be satisfied simply by taking Production Courses. You will, eventually, have to take at least a few courses in Acting, Directing, or Camera, and 3 Courses in Screenwriting.

And you'll probably want to take these classes *before* you finally get around to shooting that movie of yours. You know, the one you with color and sound. Because making a movie is a grueling and stressful experience, and if you have to take a bullshit acting, writing, or liberal arts class while you're doing it, you might just go nuts.

When I attended the program, I had an interest in directing. So I took "Actor's Craft". It turned out to be a basic acting class, where we would memorize a scene and apply different acting methods. Like using sense memory. Which is when you need to feel angry about something in a scene, you remember a time when you were really pissed off and use it bring up that emotion in the scene. I conveniently tuned into the anger I felt at not being allowed to make a real movie for two years and transformed it into a stellar performance.

It was actually a pretty fun class.

But it was 3 credits.

3 CREDITS.

Today, that is $3,444.

A THREE THOUSAND FOUR HUNDRED DOLLAR ACTING CLASS.

That's like paying five hundred bucks for a FUCKING PACK OF STARBURST.

Allow me to elaborate.

I live in Los Angeles, where you can throw a rock on the street and hit an actor. (Author's note: do not actually throw a rock on the street.) Acting classes are plentiful. Many of these classes are taught by people with Industry Experience.

And they NEVER, EVER cost more than a few hundred dollars. EVER.

Why? Because actors don't have any money. They're actors.

Also, no acting class is WORTH Three Thousand Dollars. You'd be better off spending the money on plastic surgery.

There are also directing classes available, as well as technical classes in how to better use a film and video camera. Outside of a Private Four Year University, you would never, *ever* pay Three or Four Thousand Dollars for one of these classes.

EVER.

It's an OBSCENE amount of money.

It's like:

- paying $1,000 for a box of Kleenex

- paying $500 for a bowl of cereal
- charging $5,000 for a drywall patch
- spending $15,000 on a breath mint

Even classes at Groundlings or the Upright Citizens Brigade are only $300 to $500.

How else can I illustrate this more clearly?

Ooh! Bar graph!

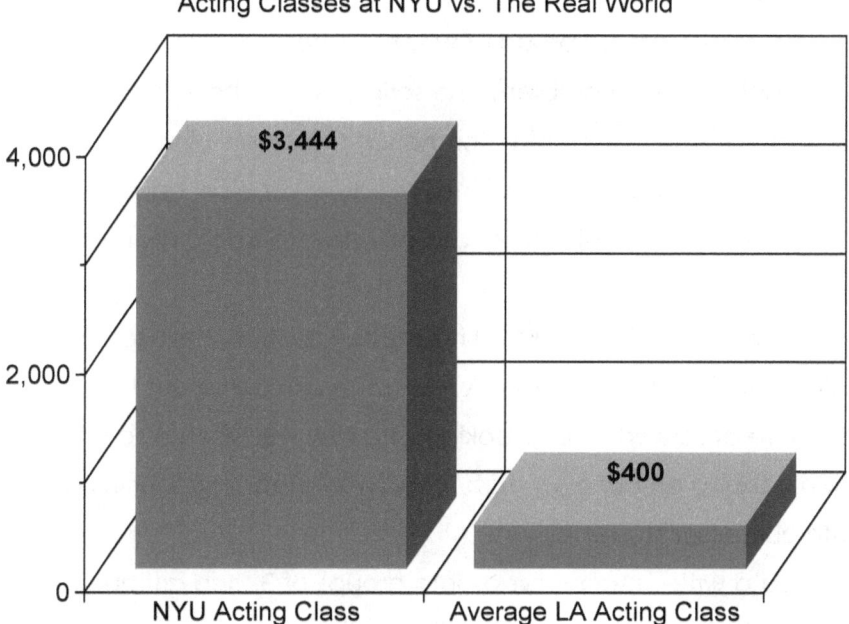

This applies to Screenwriting Classes as well. Screenwriting is not a complex art requiring years of expensive education. There are great books on screenwriting, and tons of classes on screenwriting, as well as screenwriting conventions and screenwriting contests, web sites, tutorials, DVDs, the works. Several private companies even employ former script readers from the studios, who will do coverage on your script for a hundred bucks.

But all of the growth and productivity comes from the toil of actually sitting at your computer hour after hour, day by day, and actually *doing it*.

Robert McKee's seminar is considered to be standard fare for screenwriters in the trade. I've never taken the course, but I did read his book *Story*. It is comprehensive, analytical, challenging, and thought provoking.

Unlike the courses I took at Tisch as part of the Writing requirement. I am still proud of what I wrote during these courses. There was only one problem. The scripts I wrote had dialogue and movement. This meant that, for the first two years of school, I was unable to shoot anything I wrote. Because I couldn't adapt it into black and white silent movies or slideshows, or radio dramas, or documentaries.

As with the other courses I had taken at Tisch, the Professor's "Guidance" was laughable. A few general rules about the structure of screenwriting, looking at a few well written scripts, and then working on our own stuff. Then "workshopping" our scripts with our fellow students.

You'd write a script, break into groups of 3, and critique each other's stuff. Just like every creative writing class I've ever taken. Is sharing your work and getting feedback productive? Absolutely. Did I learn things during the course? Absolutely! Were they the product of the Professor or the Cirriculum?

Absolutely not.

It was the product of interacting with other creative people. And writing. And reading. Which can be done in any screenwriting class in any venue anywhere in the world. There are writing groups. Gotham City Workshop. Community College classes. Online writing classes. They will all give you the same thing. An opportunity to learn the basics, share thoughts and ideas, and have your work seen and heard.

You're best screenwriting teachers are going to be adjuncts who work in the business. They might be able to tell you how to get a writing assistant job. But the Professors who have been there for years are usually there because they haven't sold anything in a long time.

You are required to take 3 writing classes. These classes are 4 credits each. That means the writing requirement costs you a total of $13,776. Compare that to the 10 week Screenwriting I Course at Gotham Writer's Workshop, which costs $395. If you follow up and take the Screenwriting 2 Course, and then the Master's Class, you've spent about $1,335 on 30 weeks of screenwriting classes.

$13,776 vs. $1,335.

Hmmmm. This is really getting hard to believe. Let's take a look at some of the different literature:

NYU's Introduction to Dramatic & Visual Writing H56.0031   Lecture   4 Credits

Course Level: Fundamental

Prerequisite: Sophomore status.
NOTE: STUDENT MUST ALSO REGISTER FOR ONE RECITATION.

This course is divided into lectures, seminars, and screenings of films illustrating basic aspects of screenwriting, structure, action, conflict, character development, resolution, etc. Students analyze original screenplays and write original work, including a first draft of a short screenplay. Students are expected to attend two individual conferences per semester, appointments to be arranged by the student and the instructor. This sequence is a prerequisite for all other dramatic writing courses.

Screenwriting I - Syllabus

Each week a new topic is explored through lecture and writing exercise. The topics covered in this course include:

Introduction to Screenwriting - The visual nature of movies. Screenplays as blueprints. Where to find ideas. Forming a premise. High and low concept. Hollywood vs. Indie. Genre. The usefulness of outlines.

Plot I - Finding a major dramatic question. The three-act structure. The difference between classic plots and subtle plots. Making a story map.

Character - Finding a strong protagonist. Handling other characters. Making characters dimensional through desire and contrasts. Creating character profiles. Showing characters through their actions.

Format/Description - How to format a screenplay. Writing effective screenplay description.

Scene - Scene defined. Length of scene. Tenets of a good scene-importance, desire/conflict, structure, compression, visual storytelling. Sequences. Making a step outline.

Dialogue - Dialogue's illusion of reality. Compression. Characterization through dialogue. Subtext. Exposition. Stage directions. Voice over.

Subplot - The value of subplots. Romantic subplots. Other kinds of subplots for the protagonist. Non-protagonist subplots. Subplot structure. Finding subplots in your story.

Plot II - Creating an effective opening section. Techniques for sustaining Act II. Creating an effective climax. Flashbacks.

Tone/Theme - Developing tone through genre, world, and lightness/darkness. Consistency of tone. Theme defined. Types of theme. Weaving theme into a story.

Revision - Exploration of the various stages of revision.

The Business - Creating pitches. Studios, producers, and representation. How to get your pitch to players in the industry. Query letters. The life of a screenwriter.

Note: Content may vary slightly among individual classes.

Back

Hold on a second. The NYU Course is designed for you to finish a *first draft* of a *short script*. You're going to spend 14 weeks on a SHORT SCRIPT? That's THREE MONTHS! To write something that is going to be TEN PAGES?!

Meanwhile, the less glamorous, less expensive Gotham Workshop is teaching you how to write the beginnings of a FEATURE SCRIPT. And they're also addressing the issue of pitching scripts and finding representation.

And yet, the NYU class costs $4,592. And the Gotham class, which looks like it actually covers much more ground, costs $395.

GUH?!

Let's ask the bar graph. The bar graph never lies.

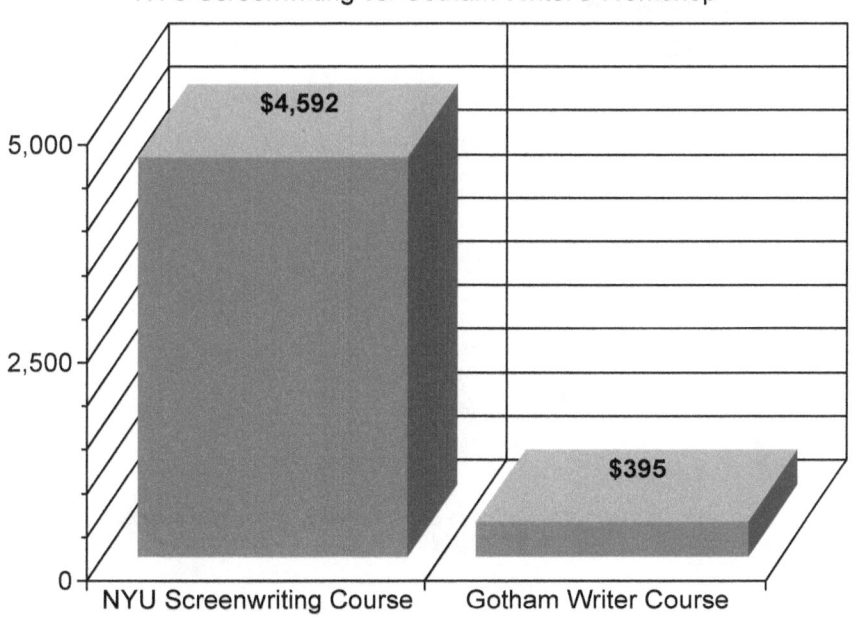

NYU Screenwriting vs. Gotham Writer's Workshop

Wow. That Gotham Writer's course must really suck. I mean, they don't even give you that magical writing dust that makes all of your ideas brilliant like when you take a class at NYU.

Hmmm. What else could justify a difference of $4,000 in these classes. Is there some kind of technical skill they bequeath to you at NYU found nowhere else?

Well, back in the day, you did have to actually learn how to format a screenplay. You know, how to indent correctly to write dialogue and locations and scene breaks and so forth. Now, you can rely on the magic of *Movie Magic Screenwriting* software, or *Final Draft*. It automatically configures and populates your screenplay with the correct format. Of course, the amazing ideas have to come from you. And that magical writing dust. Or, as we in the business call it, "Cocaine".

But the formatting is easy. Here's an example.

```
INT. NYU CLASSROOM - DAY

JOHN, 19, and BILLY, 18, sit around a wobbly wooden table,
talking about school. John holds up his 10 page script.

                    JOHN
          Do you realize that this course
          cost us $4,592?

                    BILLY
          You've got to be shitting me.
                    (MORE)
```

And remember, you can use Italics and adverbs to emphasize character emotions as well.

```
INT. NYU CLASSROOM - DAY

JOHN, 19, and BILLY, 18, sit around a wobbly wooden table,
talking about school. John holds up his 10 page script.

                    JOHN
          Do you realize that this course
          cost us $4,592?

                    BILLY
          You've got to be fucking shitting
          me.
                    (MORE)
```

Chapter 7
Producing the $100,000 Short Film

Color-Sync Workshop

H56.1040 Studio 6 Credits

Course Level: Intermediate

Prerequisites: Must have taken Sight & Sound: Film (H56.0043) and Sight & Sound: Television (H56.0050) or Sight & Sound: Studio (H56.0051) or Sight & Sound: Documentary (H56.0080). It is strongly recommended that you enroll in Post-Production Colloquium, H56.0060, 1 credit, in the same semester that you enroll in any intermediate-level core production course.

Color Sync Workshop is a practical course in which students (collaborating in crews of four) are exposed to a broad range of production techniques through production experience and class discussion. Each group produces four color sync-sound **exercises** during the semester that challenge craft, aesthetic and production issues. As a group member, each student will serve in rotation as director, producer, camera, sound, and AC/gaffer. Students are encouraged to edit their work in the Intermediate Edit Workshop (H56.1018) the following semester.

Important note: students should enter Color Sync Workshop with a short (i.e., 3-5 page) script. The production work in this course is strenuous. Students should be conscious of this when designing their semester schedules.

Wow. It's finally time. I can't believe it. Will somebody pinch me? Ow! So this isn't a dream. It's finally time to shoot that color film with synch sound! And I will finally get to realize the vision of that 3 to 5 page script I have been slaving over for the past 2 years!

That's right, a 3 to 5 page script. They do say "Brevity is the soul of wit." And at NYU Film, we strictly enforce that axiom with a pitiful little film and equipment allotment to ensure that your films will not run too long. After all, you still aren't *really* ready to make a short film. This course is still just an opportunity to engage in an *exercise*. And your first exercise is trying to figure out how to make a coherent narrative on 800 feet of film and limited camera access.

800 feet of 16mm film is about 22 minutes of total shooting time.

Two rolls of 400 feet 16mm negative cost about $100 each with a student discount. Part of your allotment also includes developing and printing these 800 feet of film. Which comes to about $336.

Plus, you have limited access to the school's battered and ancient Arri-S2 16mm film cameras. It's a crap shoot whether the particular camera you get will produce a good picture or not.

Here's a thing about the shape of these cameras. When you rent a camera from a professional establishment, you have to sign lots of insurance forms and undergo a lengthy check-in, check-out progress. It's like renting a car. The technicians make sure that the cameras are in good condition from rental to rental and, if not, the party who has manhandled the camera is held responsible, and the camera is repaired. End result: the cameras remain in good working condition over many years of time.

But at NYU, things work a little differently. For Color Synch, cameras are not inspected between shoots. Instead, students engage in what is known as an "in field" transfer. It's where one crew of students "passes on" the camera to another. The students are responsible for a little checklist of the camera's quality and shape. But since the students are only *now* beginning to use a film camera, they really aren't as well versed on their mechanics as… say… a professional technician. So the cameras end up with all sorts of problems… scratched lenses, dented assemblies, small working parts jiggled out of place. And when the cameras are finally returned to the school, it's never clear who is responsible for the damage.

The results in a lot of stupid, unnecessary drama.

And fucked up cameras.

Not to mention the fact that the school's equipment hub looks more like Doc Brown's science lab than a professional rental space. And most of the people running the check out space are students as well. I don't have anything against the students. But as you can see, the school is not exactly training them how to be great technical camera wizards. Most of them have spent 2 years making slideshows and working with tape recorders and cannot possibly have learned as much as a professional camera tech. Therefore, the equipment is simply not cared for in the manner that is should be.

But that's okay. Because this is just another *exercise*.

Of course, it is an exercise that takes 14 weeks.

That's 3 and a half months.

Your equipment allotment is for 4 days.

FOUR DAYS.

All 3 "Lord of the Rings" were shot in a year. By the time you've been in school for 2 years and 3 ½ months, you've shot a 3 to 5 minute film. I should give the school props, actually. You do get to feel a little bit like you're working on a Hollywood movie. After all, those 5 minutes of film have already cost you a total of $125,000.

The class is 6 credits. Plus that suggested "Post Production Curriculum" for another credit. Which means the whole kit-n-kaboodle is $8,036.

Yet, the school is providing you with only $536 worth of film stock and lab costs. Where does the other $7500 go?

Nobody knows. It's a mystery. Like Bigfoot or the success of Dane Cook.

And as for the camera rental? And the lighting, grip, and sound rental?

Let's say you were shooting this short, short, short film on your own. You'd be hard pressed to find an Arri-S 2 Camera, because well… it's obsolete. Most rental houses carry the Arri-S 3 line of 16 mm cameras. After some considerable research, I did find a rental house in Cincinnati that rents Arri-S 2's for $240 a day. But if you were to go with Abel Cine Tech or another NYC based reputable rental house, you'd have to go with the more advanced Arri S-3 or Aaton XTRProd. These babies rent for $350 a day.

Now, when you rent anything in the film business for more than a few days, the daily rate will go down. It's just the nature of commerce. So, technically, renting one of these new, far superior cameras for a week would cost you $350 times 4 days which equals $1,400. But once you negotiate a better quote, it should be less than that.

You should pay attention, because chances are that you will end up renting an outside camera. Most students do. Mostly because:

    a.) The time the school's camera is available may not work
        with your shooting schedule
    b.) Most of the school's cameras are shit

When I shot my Color Synch project back in 1998, I rented an Aaton Super 16mm camera from Abel Cine Tech. My DP worked out a deal where it cost me $1,000 for the week. I also had to rent a Cargo Van for the grip equipment and purchase several extra rolls of film. Back then, the allotment was 400 feet of film. Which meant 11 minutes of shooting.

How did the allotment increase from 400 to 800 feet?

According to recent graduates, there were so many complaints from the student body about the piss poor allotment that the Professors, tired of all the whining, decided to prove the students wrong by make their own film using only the 400 feet. A Camera Professor was the Director of Photography. A Writing Professor wrote the script. A Directing Professor Directed. An Editing Professor Edited.

They planned it out and shot.

And they failed miserably.

They had to do what every student taking Color Synch does. Spring for more film, more camera time, and go well well beyond the school's pathetic allotment.

So, they acquiesced some and increased the allotment to 800 feet.

The school provides you with battered grip, lighting, and sound equipment. If you were to rent lights, some basic grip equipment, plus a sound recorder and shotgun mic on your own, it would probably run you another five hundred or thousand bucks, if that.

Ultimately, outside of the school, you could shoot for a full week using brand new, top of the line film equipment for less than $3,000. And that includes film stock and developing. Yet this class, which provides you with outdated cameras, inferior equipment, and very little film stock, costs you $8,036.

I've heard from recent students that the school *intentionally* makes the allotment so small in order to "sharpen production skills". The idea being that if you force somebody to work with less than what is required, they will rise to the task and creatively problem solve under the gun.

That kind of makes sense. Independent filmmaking is fraught with endless obstacles which do require you to problem solve and work with what is available. You may encounter situations in the working world where you have to shoot what should be a $20,000 commercial with a $10,000 budget. And it's important to know how to work with limited resources.

But paying someone $8,036 to work with limited resources? That's stupid.

Are You Smarter Than a High Schooler?

Another problem within the elitist, academic environment of Tisch is the continual snubbing of video. Even when I was a student, there was a high brow argument against the use of video for "true artistic expression". Video cameras were limited to use in Experimental and TV classes.

The quality of Digital Video increases every year. As does the accessibility. And proportionally, the cost *deceases*. Which is what film snobs, like the academics at Tisch, really hate. Because it has rendered their institution obsolete.

As I have mentioned, you could assemble your own video studio complete with professional camera, lights, grip, editing, and sound equipment for less than the cost of 2 classes at Tisch.

The cost of professional video has become so low that Tisch has actually introduced video into some of their upper level production courses. But still, the school does not offer any introductory narrative video classes early in the curriculum. When it comes time for Color Synch, you've never actually had the opportunity, within the school, to make a narrative project with color and sound. Your first foray into this world comes when you are using *film*. Film is WAY more expensive than video.

So you are going to make a ton of mistakes, like anybody trying something for the first time. But they are going to be very, very expensive and unnecessary mistakes.

Most students will not stick to the 3 to 5 minute "suggested" run time of a Color Synch project for a few reasons. First off, 2 years of pent up creativity cannot be adequately expressed in such a short project. Secondly, each Student knows that he came to this school to make movies, not exercises, even if the Administration does not.

It's funny that the school does not offer a Freshman Year video course where students simply learn basic lighting, sound, and editing and make their own movies. As I mentioned earlier, my high school has a pretty nice A/V department that teaches the fundamentals. And Tisch even offers a pretty comprehensive summer program for high school students.

When I was a Junior, I spent the summer teaching a group of high schoolers how to shoot and edit Broadcast Video. It was kind of like summer camp, but at NYU Film. It lasted about 5 weeks. The kids didn't have to worry about anything other than their projects. No liberal arts classes. No mandatory fundamentals class. We taught them the basics, helped them find news stories, and sent them out on the town.

They produced some amazing, professional looking segments, then proceeded to put together their own on-air broadcast from the 12th Floor Studios at Tisch.

It was, overall, a pretty rewarding and amazing experience. Many of the students got really excited to apply to NYU so they could make some more stuff.

I can only imagine how baffling their first year of school would be. Imagine, you spend your summer before college working with professional video equipment and producing completed news segments. You learn to write, edit, light, record sound, operate a switcher and a TV Studio camera. You do all of this in under 3 months, for less money than a semester of tuition at the University.

Then, you are admitted to NYU Film. And you don't touch a camera your first 2 semesters. And your second year, you re-learn over a period of 14 weeks what you were taught 2 years earlier in 5 weeks, for about 10 times the amount of money.

Buh?

Chapter 8
Working for Free and Paying to Work

If you track down any graduate from any film school and ask them for any advice, they will inevitably say this:

"Forget about class. Just Crew. And Intern. Shoot stuff."

Now, this is good advice. But it brings up a larger quandary. Allow me to explain.

"Crewing" simply means "work on other people's film shoots". You could be the Sound Recordist, who records sound. Or a Gaffer, who helps set up the lights. Or a Grip, who also works with lights and electricity. You could simply be a Production Assistant, who helps carry stuff and fetches lunch and does all sorts of random stuff. You could be a Camera Assistant, helping the Camera Operator and the Director of Photography. Heck, you could even *be* the Director of Photography.

You will learn more one day on a film set than you will during your entire four years of film school.

As you get more comfortable on a film set, you'll figure out what position you like best. All you need is some *basic knowledge* about what you are doing and a willingness to work and contribute.

That's it.

Now, here's the thing. You can "work on other people's film shoots"... for free. Want to be a Production Assistant? Great! Come on to the set and lend a hand. You'll learn from moment one, whether the production is run well or everything is out of control. Just hit up craigslist or mandy.com or myspace or whatever. Heck, many of the postings I see on craigslist looking for help are student films anyway.

Why pay to go to school and work on student films when you can just... work on them? They pay the same: nothing. But at least just going out and crewing won't cost you $25,000 a semester in tuition and housing.

Don't believe me?

I just hopped on the internet and found this:

35mm Bollywood Style Student Film Seeks Crew

new york craigslist > manhattan > crew gigs   email this posting to a friend

35mm Bollywood Style Student Film Seeks Crew

please flag with care:

miscategorized

prohibited

spam/overpost

best of craigslist

Reply to: gigs-412176089@craigslist.org
Date: 2007-09-02, 2:09PM EDT

"Arranged" is a 35mm NYU Undergrad senior thesis film. We are currently seeking crew members.

Who We Need:

- Assistant Camera
- Gaffer
- Grip and Electric
- Production Assistants
- Production Designer
- Make-up Artists

What We're Shooting:
- 35mm Film
- Bollywood Style Musical
- Will Look Fantastic on Any Reel

Where:
- Throughout the New York City area

When:
- September 20th - October 2nd, 2007

How to Contact Us:
- Reply to this ad immediately! Your reel will thank you for it!

While we are shooting on a small budget, we can consider paying a very reduced fee if you can justify it to us. We look forward to working with you and building your reel in outstanding ways.

- Location: New York City
- it's NOT ok to contact this poster with services or other commercial interests
- Compensation: transportation, a copy of the finished film and relevant extra footage for your reel - on 35mm!!

Wow! An NYU Senior Thesis Film! You could be a Production Assistant. Probably a Camera Assistant, too, even if you've never touched a camera. Just help out the camera guy. When it comes time to shoot a student film, the director is grateful for any help he or she can get.

But okay, maybe you don't yet have the experience or confidence to be a Camera Assistant or Grip. Then just help out as a Production Assistant. You will learn a hell of a lot, make some new friends and contacts, and you'll have something to put on your resume and reel.

If you still want be a Grip or Boom Operator but don't go have the necessary experience, then you might want to help out these guys.

NYU Senior Thesis Film seeks crew for THIS WEEKEND

new york craigslist > manhattan > crew gigs   email this posting to a friend

NYU Senior Thesis Film seeks crew for THIS WEEKEND

please flag with care:

miscategorized

prohibited

Reply to: gigs-402554724@craigslist.org
Date: 2007-08-21, 4:03PM EDT

spam/overpost

best of craigslist

"#9," a comedy shooting on 35mm film THIS WEEKEND, August 24th through the 26th, is still seeking crew! Please call 561.222.0403 for more information on the following positions:

Gaffer (some compensation provided, prior experience needed)

NO EXPERIENCE NECESSARY for:
Grips
PAs!!!!!
Make-up
Boom operator

- it's NOT ok to contact this poster with services or other commercial interests
- Compensation: no pay

PostingID: 402554724

Copyright © 2007 craigslist, inc.   terms of use   privacy policy   feedback forum

Or these guys, if you live in LA:

UCLA Thesis Short (Shoots Next Week) Needs CAMERA ASSISTANT and GRIP

los angeles craigslist > westside-southbay > crew gigs

email this posting to a friend

UCLA Thesis Short (Shoots Next Week) Needs CAMERA ASSISTANT and GRIP

Reply to: gigs-427178325@craigslist.org
Date: 2007-09-20, 4:34AM PDT

please flag with care:

miscategorized

prohibited

spam/overpost

best of craigslist

UCLA MFA director's thesis short film needs CAMERA ASSISTANT who will also act as a second camera operator for some scenes; and GRIP for 6-day shoot at UCLA and Culver City locations between Tuesday 9/25 and Sun 9/30. If interested, please reply to this craigslist ad with experience listed and email/phone contact. Candidates with limited experience encouraged to apply (just so you know what you're doing and have some experience -- no matter how small - feel free to apply)

- Location: Culver City/UCLA Locations
- it's NOT ok to contact this poster with services or other commercial interests
- Compensation: Negotiable. Please contact for more info.

PostingID: 427178325

Copyright © 2007 craigslist, inc.   terms of use   privacy policy   feedback forum

Now, if you'll flip back to the course description for "Frame and Sequence", you will see that as part of the class you are encouraged to put in at least 12 hours of crewing on a Senior Level project. And that is excellent advice.

But why pay $4,592 to do it?

Why?

Why?!

...*for the love of God*...

Why??!??!!!!!!

A Conversation Between 2 NYU Film Grads

Seth: "So did you learn much in the NYU Film Program?"

Veronica: "No."

Seth: "So would you have skipped college then?"

Veronica: "Well no, an education is really important."

Seth: "But has the degree helped you find work?"

Veronica: "No."

Seth: "Did the professors help you learn more about your craft?"

Veronica: "Not really."

Seth: "Did you ever get a job interview or a special opportunity because of your degree or your time in the school?"

Veronica: "No."

Seth: "So why would you do it again if you had the choice?"

Veronica: "Well, because having an education is important. It expanded my mind."

Seth: "How exactly did it expand your mind?"

Veronica: "Well some of the non film classes I took very really interesting. They made me think differently about the world."

Seth: "Okay. Were they worth the price of tuition?"

Veronica: "Heck no! $30,000 a year?! *(that's what we paid back in 1997)* Are you nuts?!"

Seth: "So, if you could do it again would you skip it?"

Veronica: "Well no, having a degree is really important."

Seth: "How, exactly?"

Veronica: "Well, to be part of an intelligent society, you need to be educated."

Seth: "Do you feel what you learned in school helped you be part of an intelligent society?"

Veronica: "Well, not the school exactly. But during that time, I was questioning things, and I learned a lot."

Seth: "From your classes."

Veronica: "No, more from my life experiences. I grew as a person."

Seth: "Okay, so why was being in a classroom in a school paying all this money and getting a piece of paper that says you graduated so important?"

Veronica: "Well, you know, Seth, having an education is really important. It's invaluable."

Seth: "What do you mean? Like you can't put a price on it?"

Veronica: "Well, yeah."

Seth: "But they do put a price on it. $1,148 a point, to be exact."

Veronica: "Well, that's just the school having to function in this… consumerist society."

Seth: "So, what, the school is the victim now?"

Veronica: "Well, you can't really put a price on education."

Seth: "Yes, you can. $1,148 a point times 128 points equals about $146,944.00. Without housing."

Veronica: "That's not what I mean. I mean you need college no matter how much it costs."

Seth: "Like crack."

Veronica: "Shut up."

Internships

Interns are college students who work for free at a company in exchange for college credit. Being an intern is just like being a bitch in prison. Except that you aren't abused physically, just mentally and psychologically. And it costs you more money.

Every field has interns. In film, interns do grunt work, make coffee, pick up lunch, pick up dry cleaning, plunge toilets (I did this), hole punch papers, courier tapes, and anything else you can think of that nobody wants to do.

However, the experience can actually be quite beneficial. Just as being a prison bitch gives you a "Husband" who protects you and teaches you about life on the inside, being an office bitch gives you a Supervisor who can teach you a lot about making coffee.

When I was a Junior, I interned at the then fledgling Fox News Channel. I worked in their Sports department, where I logged tapes and filed stuff and typed and whatever else kind of things around the office needed done. Sometimes I would bring important tapes or files from the 26th floor down into the basement.

After reviewing my transcript, I realize that this internship took care of 6 credits towards my degree.

$6,888 by today's standards.

Ga-buh-buh!

Seven thousand dollars to make photocopies. And file.

Most of my supervisors at Fox were cocks. But one guy was really cool. He helped me put together my own news story. I decided to write one about shorter than average athletes like Mugsy Bouges and Wayne Crebet and Theo Fleury.

Theo Fluery is a hockey player who spent most of his career with the Calgary Flames. But when I was at Fox, he was with the

New York Rangers. So this supervisor let me call Madison Square Garden, arrange an interview, and check out a camera van and rig for the day. We went into the Ranger's locker room and I got to interview one of my hockey heroes. He's only 5'5" but thick as a truck. And he gave a great interview.

It was awesome.

Unfortunately, the douschebags that run the department found out about the interview. It turns out I was not authorized to engage in such an educational undertaking. I was but a lowly intern and I might have said something stupid to embarrass Fox. How anyone could possibly embarrass the Fox network is beyond me.

Anyway, my cool supervisor got in trouble and I wasn't allowed to finish the segment. I went back to my more noble intern work of filing shit and what not.

Eventually, I applied to work at Fox as a News Editor and was hired as a freelancer. (Which means low pay and no benefits). I had achieved the one thing every college graduate dreams of: some kind of income. It made me the think that film school might have been worthwhile.

There's only one other thing.

I wasn't the only intern at Fox. I had buddies from other colleges.

State Schools.

Community Colleges I had never heard of.

Colleges that cost MUCH MUCH LESS.

They were interning the same place I was. They ended up getting hired as editors just like me.

But *none* of them was stupid enough to pay $7,000 for the privilege.

I do think internships can be valuable. If you happen to be enrolled in an affordable college. In my case, I had just paid $100K plus to get a job paying less than $30,000 a year, with no health insurance. On the plus side, I did learn how to write a well reasoned essay. Actually, I already knew how to do that from high school. In fact, I had to write well reasoned essays to be admitted into college. But... whatever, who has time to think about this kind of thing. It's only money. Geesh. I am so materialistic.

Besides, there are plenty of companies in the film industry who would be happy to hire you for free without college credit.

There are so many people trying desperately to work in the film business that it has lowered the paying wage considerably. The people in charge can say they are looking for someone with "lots of energy" and a "self starter" to work for nothing with the dream of eventually getting hired.

After a few months of job hunting in Los Angeles, I came across a non paying intern position in development at a small production company. The position would have involved working on scripts, doing coverage (reading scripts and determining if they are good or not), and pitching story ideas to executives. The guys who ran the company created MTV's "Fear", a very popular TV show a few years ago.

I called up a friend at NYU's Office of Career Development. I asked him what he thought of an opportunity like this. He told me that the school warned all graduates against working in non paying positions after school.

Ironically, I found out that the guys who were hiring for this position actually graduated from NYU Film.

Now, I can understand the school's stance on not doing work for free after you've graduated. In theory, your spending 4 years inside their Academic program should give you the right to just move into paying work.

But that's not how it works.

The sad truth is, even after you've earned your prestigious degree and sent out hundreds of resumes, you probably won't have a job. You will find yourself in line with everyone else to get a "foot in the door", which means doing work for free or next to nothing.

You're in the exact same boat as everyone else.

Except that you've got more debt.

You are also under prepared with unrealistically inflated expectations and no money.

But don't worry, your school hasn't forgotten you. Just wait. When things are at their darkest, they will give you a call to see how you are doing.

Chapter 9
Salt in the Wounds

Your Untimely Death

Within a year of graduation, you will receive solicitations from the school's fundraising department. Usually the caller will be a 3rd year Acting or Film Student working for $9 an hour, completely oblivious to the financial hole they are digging themselves into.

These calls can be very difficult to take.

You want so badly to *give back* to the school for everything they've given you. But how can you possibly repay a debt for something as enriching as an education? I mean besides the $390 a month for the student loans. These people provided you with the skills and connections you needed to get that job as a runner over at Mark Burnett Productions working for $10 an hour. You want to make sure that future generations have the same opportunity to reap the benefits of this high quality education, so that someday they too can buy lunch at a Santa Monica deli for their boss before rushing out again to get his dry cleaning.

You may not have much left to give after paying rent and car insurance and what not. But I know you will find a way. Just skip one of those unnecessary expenditures here and there. Who needs dinner anyways? It's an overrated meal. And who needs socks? Really, they're offensive. Like condoms for your feet. Saving on extravagances like these can really add up! Perhaps you can even give plasma or collect soda cans. Eventually, you'll have enough to make a respectable donation.

Now I know what you're thinking. You're thinking, "Seth, what if I die, due to a perilous film shoot or lack of health insurance? How will I continue to make donations to my school?"

Fear not. Tisch runs this ad in every alumni newsletters:

> # Leave a Legacy to Tisch
>
> Your annual support is important to the Tisch School. By including Tisch in your will, you can ensure that your support continues beyond your lifetime. You can use the following language to provide a legacy to Tisch in your will: "I give, devise and bequeath [assets] to New York University, 70 Washington Square South, New York, New York 10012, for the use of the Tisch School of the Arts." Please contact us for draft language if you would like to establish a permanent named fund, such as a scholarship fund, through your legacy. When you name Tisch in your estate plans, the University will recognize your special generosity you during your lifetime by enrolling you in The Society of The Torch. To learn more, contact the NYU Office of Gift Planning at 212.998.6960 or e-mail us at gift.planning@nyu.edu.

So hurry up and get famous, then die. You will be fondly remembered by your school, so long as you cut a nice check before you go.

Narrative Workshop

H56.1245   Studio   4 Credits

Course Level: Advanced

Course is repeatable two times for 8 total points.
Prerequisites: Color Sync Workshop (H56.1040), or Documentary Workshop (H56.1041), or Experimental Workshop (H56.1046), or Intermediate Television (H56.1077), or Children's Television Production Workshop (H56.1222) or Broadcast Documentary (H56.1080), or Intermediate Animation (H56.1329).

This workshop is a practical course in which students work collaboratively in crews of four to produce up to seven 16mm dramatic films. Each student works on one film in one basic crew role (Director, Producer, Camera, Sound, **Art Direction**), but is exposed to a broad spectrum of production experience itself. Problems in directing, staging shots, sound design, and editing are explored. Dailies are discussed in seminar meetings. All aspects of production are viewed as a creative extension and continuation of the film writing process. Students *interested in directing* in this class must be prepared to submit a script on the first class of the term.

Selected scripts will be chosen in class. Script parameters are the following:

1. 12 pages in length
2. Fewer than 4 main characters (prefer 2)
3. No more than 2 major locations.

Note: Films produced for Narrative Workshop will not be eligible for awards in the First Run Film Festival if they are longer than 15 minutes, including titles. All films produced in Narrative will be screened if entered in the First Run Festival, but those longer than 15 minutes will not be judged.

You are finally a second semester Junior. You are ready to take those elite, high level production courses that you've been dreaming of since you were a Freshman. You will finally have the chance produce a real short film of 5 to 12 minutes in length.

Well, maybe. Kind of.

"Narrative Workshop", which is described above, only allows for 10 directors and allotments per semester. Your class will probably have between 20 and 30 students. That means that you have roughly a 1 out of 3 chance of getting to direct. It's up to your Professor. And if he likes you or not.

I know that may not seem fair. But consider this: just because you paid the school to teach you to make films, and make films, does that mean you should actually get to make films?

Think about it.

Truthfully, the school is helping teach you a very, very valuable lesson about the film industry. Not everybody gets to make a movie. So if you are one of the 20 students in a Narrative class who does not have a chance to write or direct, you are actually *ahead* of your classmates who are helming their own projects.

And this lesson only cost another $4,592.

If the price is getting too steep, I'll cut you a deal. You can just pay me just $2,000, and I will not let you make a movie. I'm very good at not letting people make movies. Not as good as NYU, but pretty good.

You, Student; You, Magician!

What's this? You have been chosen by the mighty Professor to direct? How wonderful! This truly validates your worth as a filmmaker, and as a human being. Aren't you glad that you've subjected yourself to an autocratic system of selective self expression? You truly are a better person than your classmates. How satisfying!

So now you are making a 10 to 15 minute film. That's almost twice to three times as long as the Color Synch film. If you'll recall, the school gave you about $536 worth of materials to make your short 3 to 5 minute film. 800 feet of film plus 800 feet worth of lab developing time. All in all you got to shoot about 22 minutes of footage.

Naturally, since this class is more advanced, you should have more materials to work with.

Not!

Only *losers* make a movie with an adequate amount of equipment, film stock, and lab fees. You're better than that. No, to make sure that you truly hone your elite filmmaking skills, you're going to have to make a movie twice as long as your Color Synch... with *almost the same amount of materials!*

Wow!

Check it out:

Narrative Workshop

H56.1245

> 10 Students direct one project each on 16mm film, up to 15 minutes in length, sync sound or MOS, color or B&W.

SUPPLIES

Allotments are given in the form of a check, in the amount of $800.00, which must be picked up during the semester in which you are taking the class*. Final print allotments will be distributed at the discretion of a faculty committee. *Allotment checks cannot be processed during the summer.* *NYU PRODUCTION INSURANCE: Available only with instructor approval.

PRODUCTION EQUIPMENT

2 class rigs scheduled in "slots" of time composed of 5 shooting days plus 1 check-out day and 1 check-in day. Each selected production is guaranteed 1 slot. Shooting slots are either Tuesday-to-Tuesday or Thursday-to-Thursday. *See the following page for a list of available equipment.*

The Narrative Workshop Allotment provides no film stock or lab vouchers. It *does* provide you with a check for EIGHT HUNDRED DOLLARS for you to buy your own! That's roughly equivalent to $300 *more* than the amount of film and lab fees you got for Color Synch! You know what that means? 11 MORE MINUTES of footage!

Plus, you get the camera rig for FIVE days instead of FOUR, like in Color Synch. That's a WHOLE EXTRA DAY! YAY!

That seems to make sense. In fact, I think that perhaps the people who run Tisch are just misunderstood geniuses. Like Ross Perot or Q-Bert.

Color Sync Workshop
H56.1040

Students form crews of 4. Each student directs one, 3-8 minute, color, sync-sound exercise on 16mm film. Each student also shoots, produces, and records sound for their crew mates.

SUPPLIES

- Film stock: 800' of 16mm color negative
- Processing: 800' normal developing and one-lite video transfer (lab voucher)
- 1 65-min DAT Tape
- 1 60-min Beta Tape
- 1 30-min Beta Tape
- 1 roll of Gaffer Tape
- 1 roll of Camera Tape
- 10 CD-R's

Now for some reason Narrative is only 4 credits, which means it only costs $4,592 as opposed to Color Synch's 6 credits for $6,888. So you're paying less money for a more advanced class where you're making a longer movie with a smaller ratio of materials.

Unless you poop film stock, you are going to have to buy more. Lots more. And if you *can* poop film stock...then you should see a doctor. Because that isn't natural.

$800 can buy you 1200 feet of film and developing. How exactly does the school expect you to make a 15 minute movie with only 33 minutes of footage? Do they think you are Jesus Spielberg, endowed not only with a keen aesthetic eye and vivid imagination, but the ability to control life and weather?

During a shoot, your actors will flub lines. The camera will jam. Somebody will trip and fall. The sun will come out during a shot. It's the nature of filmmaking. You need a few takes to get a scene right, unless you are Clint Eastwood.

All movies start out with a ton more footage than what you see up on the screen. That's what editing is for.

You're supposed to be learning how to make movies. Learning means making mistakes, which means room for error. But as soon as you complete the dunderheaded Fundamentals requirements and enroll yourself in a real moviemaking class, you're competing with your fellow students for dibs on directing.

Congratulations, you've just graduated from Kindergarten to "American Idol". With shitty microphones. And Simon Cowell is peeing on you.

Mo' Money! Mo' Money! Mo' Money!

You are now a Senior. You've invested $150,000 into your education, and you're asking yourself, "How can I waste more money?"

I suppose you could light the money on fire. Or dump it into a bottomless pit. Or a moderately deep pit with a dragon at the bottom. Or make thousands of tiny paper airplanes. But maybe those suggestions are a little too radical. I understand. We'll stay within your comfort zone. We'll stick to wasting your money on ridiculous film classes.

Have I got a course for you!

"Advanced Production Workshop" is an opportunity for you to take a class that spans TWO semesters. That's an entire year to make a 15 to 30 minute film! You're allotment is $1,600. That's twice as much money, and twice as much time, as your Narrative! The course costs twice as much, and lasts twice as long.

You're even given 2 shooting slots of 12 days each.
Wow.
That's 24 days to use up roughly 66 minutes of film stock.
You'd better work slowly. Really slowly. And you'd better not make any mistakes! You've only got 36 extra minutes to work with.

Ha ha! Just kidding. But seriously, you're gonna have to buy more film stock. Again. And you're going to have to rent more grip equipment and pay more lab fees. Again. And probably rent a better camera. Again. Like you would, normally, even if you weren't in film school. But aren't you glad that you are?

Advanced Productions have been known to cost anywhere from $10,000 to $50,000 on top of tuition. And that's also on top of any extra money you've put into your Color Synch or Narratives.

As before, only 10 students out of a class of 30 gets to direct. Guess what happens to those 20 other students who get shit canned? They enroll in Narrative Workshop to compete with the younger students for the right to direct! That's why Narrative is so overcrowded.

If you don't get to direct, guess what? You get to spend 2 semesters and $9,184 crewing.

Advanced Production Workshop

H56.1054

10 students direct one narrative or experimental project each on 16mm film up to 30 minutes in length, sync sound or MOS, color or black & white. Registration for the class is by permission of the instructor. This is a two semester class, Fall/Spring or Spring/Fall.

SUPPLIES

Allotments are given in the form of a check, in the amount of $1,600.00, which must be picked up during the semester. Final print allotments will be distributed at the discretion of a faculty committee. Final print allotments will be distributed at the discretion of a faculty committee. *Allotment checks cannot be processed during the summer.* *NYU PRODUCTION INSURANCE:* Available only with instructor approval.

PRODUCTION EQUIPMENT

1 class rig scheduled in "slots" of time composed of 12 shooting days plus 1 check out day and 1 check in day. Each student is guaranteed 2 shooting slots. Shooting slots are Wednesday to Wednesday. *See the following page for a list of available equipment.*

FORMATS:

16mm (ArriSR), Super 16mm (ArriSR), HD (Panasonic HVX200), 24p (Panasonic AJ-DVX100)
16mm – *Scheduled through instructor*
Super16mm, HD, 24p – *Scheduled through Faculty Head of Production Studies (Rick Litvin) on a first come, first served basis.*

Now, if you do get into this class and get chosen to direct, but don't happen to have another $10,000 to $50,000 lying around the house, you *may* want to consider shooting your project on video.

Shooting on video saves you the cost of paying for expensive film stock and lab fees. And now that you've paid your dues, you have access to some of the industry's most cutting edge technology.

The Panasonic DVX100, 24p Camcorder:

The Panasonic AG-DVX100 24p camcorder is available to students in **Advanced-level production courses only** (Narrative, Advanced Experimental, Advanced Production, Broadcast Doc., Narrative TV) as a replacement for the standard production camera. It is approved and coordinated by the Executive Director of Production Studies, Prof. Rick Litvin. The camera is available on a first come, first served basis.

Due to limited supply, camera tests for approved projects must be done in-house in the Production Center.

Post Production Concerns for the 24p: During principle photography, students are advised to shoot in 24p Standard mode, to maintain consistency in the edit and to avoid problems such as dropped frames.

The Panasonic DVX-100 is a 3 chip 1/3" CCD camera with great picture and sound capabilities. It's lightweight, versatile, and durable. Its innovative 24p mode produces a picture that emulates the motion quality of film. It completely redefined the world of independent filmmaking.

Five years ago.

Today, many students receive this camera as a graduation present. You probably have a friend that owns one. It's not that expensive. Check it out:

Panasonic.

Panasonic AG-DVX100B 3-CCD 24p/30p/60i Mini-DV Cinema Camcorder, NTSC, with CineSwitch Technology, CineGamma Software, FireWire Interface and New Black Sapphire Color

Mfr# AGDVX100B • B&H# PAAGDVX100B

6 Customer Reviews   Price: $ 2,649.95

That's less than the price of one class at Tisch!

If you don't have the cash to buy one, because you've blown it on tuition, you can rent one fairly cheaply. Most of the uppity rental houses still charge $150 a day for this camera, but there are a number of smaller outfits that offer great deals. I like these guys who are located in LA, at www.hdpioneers.com. Check this out:

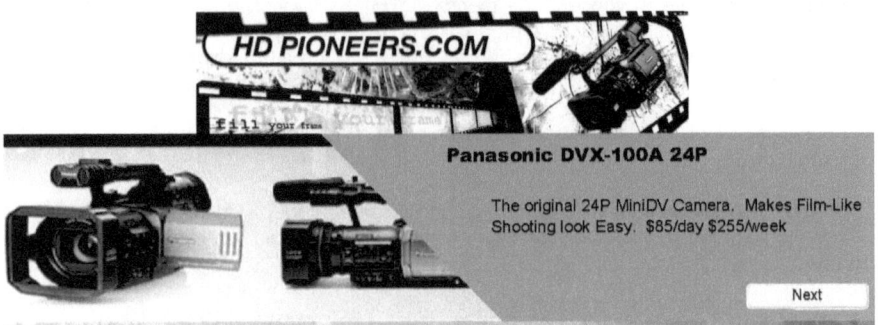

Oh. Remember that class at Glendale Community College that only costs $60? You know, the one where you learn basic lighting and sound then get access to a video camera and digital editing equipment for the semester?

Yeah. That one. The one that costs Sixty Bucks.

This is the camera they use in that class.

That Camera. The Panasonic DVX-100a. Same thing.

Sixty bucks. No shit.

Now, to their credit, Tisch does own a few Panasonic HVX-200 HD cameras. Glendale Community College doesn't own any of those. Not yet. I think they are getting some in next semester.

It warms my heart that Tisch can stay one step ahead of a small town community college's audio visual department.

My Time as a Zombie

During Junior year, John Dickerson invited me upstate to play a Zombie in his horror short. The details of my role were never made clear, save for my character's inevitable bloody demise and some potential limb chewing/growling. It promised to be a good weekend.

I hitched a ride in a U-Haul with John's Director of Photography. We ended up in a beautiful small town called Kingston. By midday, I was shirtless in the 40 degree wind. I couldn't see the crew, the abandoned barn, or my co-star wielding a gun. The make-up artist had instructed me to keep my eyes clothes as she applied copious amounts of blue green zombie face paint. Eventually, I was allowed to open my eyes. People kept walking up to me and nodding their approval.

"He looks like a zombie."

I was handed a prosthetic arm with some fake blood on it and told to "chew, but with feeling." Then one of the PA's handed me a plastic packet of fake blood.

"Put this in your mouth."

I was told that the heroine, Jessica, would fire a gun at me and I was to scream, growl, fall down, die, bite the blood capsule, and then allow the blood to drip out of my mouth.

"Is this stuff toxic?" I asked.

John shook his head. Not a "no, of course not" shake, but a "how the hell should I know?" kind of shake.

"Um, I don't thinks so, just... try not to swallow it," he said. I didn't find this encouraging.

The crew was ready very quickly, and without so much as a rehearsal, we were rolling.

"Action!" shouted John.

I stumbled forward holding the prosthetic arm like it was a Double Double In n Out burger.

"Raaarrr! Raaaar!" I growled, and then began gnawing on the arm. I looked up. There was Jessica, pointing the gun at me. I dropped the arm and started towards her.

"Raaaa-!"

Then she shot off the gun.

I thought it was going to be a cap gun. But apparently, they were using a real gun with blanks. The fucking thing was louder than anything I had ever heard, and it scared the shit out of me.

I didn't need to act. I literally fell backwards onto the ground, skinned my knee, banged my head. But, to my credit, I stayed in character, and managed a few more "Raaarrrr!"s before biting the capsule of blood and letting my eyes close in dramatic fashion and the red liquid seeped out of my mouth.

"And.... Cut!" shouted John.

The crew cheered. The shot had been amazing. They quickly moved on to the next location, leaving me stunned, bloody, and with a mouthful of possibly toxic fake blood. I felt satisfied as an artist and rushed off to clean up.

I never did get to see the movie. But throughout the rest of the semester, random people would come up to me and tell me I was a great Zombie.

This experience was a highlight.

Part 4: Graduation and Beyond

So you've graduated from film school! Congratulations, you are four years behind everyone else in your field. But at least, for one day, you get to wear a cap and gown and march down an aisle to classical music and let the school's President hand you a piece of paper with some calligraphy on it, then get drunk and pass out in the pantry.

As you shake the President's hand, remember this: during the ceremony, he just made $829 and change. Just sitting there. How? By earning a salary of $862,717 a year. At least that's what President John Sexton was making back in 2004. It's probably more by now. Breaking that down into a typical work week, he's banking $16,590 every 5 days.

Now to be fair, I should mention that this calculation is based on his gross earnings before taxes. After the government takes its piece, he only walks home with about $9,000 a week.

How the hell is a college President supposed to live on only $9,000 a week?! The poor guy is only making $218 an hour. Which is roughly what you'll be making in a week when you graduate, if you're lucky.

Chapter 10
Life In The Inner Circle

Now what about those amazing *networking connections* you've gotten from NYU? Aren't there just hundreds of agents and studio executives waiting to meet with you and see your student films because you graduated from this prestigious school?

Well, let's see. Take a look at this.

```
================================================
In this Alumni List Serve Correspondence you will find the following
announcements:

1.  Alum seeking advice on Writer's Assistant/Reading opportunities in
LA
2.  Show Announcement
_____

1.  ALUM SEEKING ADVICE ON WRITER'S ASSISTANT/READING OPPORTUNITIES IN
LA

Hi Kelsey.  I was reading the post of another Tisch alum seeking advice
from fellow alumni on the best ways to find Writer's Assistant/Reading
opportunities.  I am also extremely interested.  I have been in LA for
almost a year and have not quite been able to make much progress as far
as
these types of opportunities are concerned.  If anyone has any advice
for
me that would be greatly appreciated.

Sincerely,

████████████
TSOA DWP/UGFTV 00'
```

This is a sampling of NYU's Tisch List-Serve. It's kind of like craigslist, but for NYU grads only. The school's promotional material indicates that it connects you with a powerful network of Tisch Alumni who are just dying to bring you into the inner circle of the film industry.

But mostly, there's just a lot of postings like this. Clueless grads looking for some kind of guidance. Lame job postings. Sometimes, they even repost job listings from a bunch of other websites. Like you haven't been on Varietycareers.com and TimeWarner.com every day since graduation. Thank God you paid $200,000 to your school so they could compile a list of job opportunities from other web sites.

If you know your shit technically and work hard, network, you will find work. It's Los Angeles. There are tons and tons of productions being shot here every day.

Will NYU help you get work on those productions?

No.

Here's what NYU can help you with:

Subject: 10/5(NY): Job Ops

Date: Fri, 05 Oct 2007 16:47:20 -0400

```
10/5 (NY) Job Ops
*********************************************************************
In this Alumni List Serve Correspondence you will find
the following Job Ops

1. Editor - Overground Films
2. Temporary Office Assistant  - Nobu
3. sound operator (one time job) - short film
4. Administrative Assistant-Investment Banking - Advantage Human
   Resourcing
5. Reception-Conference Coordinator - Advantage Human Resourcing
6. Production Coordinator - Strand Communications
*********************************************************************
```

This is the kind of motley selection of jobs that comes through the List Serve. A documentary editing position, a $10 an hour office assistant job. A sound operator gig. A job in Investment Banking. Followed by two reception/coordination positions.

I do have enormous respect of the people who actually work in the Office of Career Development. They have been fighting with the administration for years to get:

1.) More money

2.) More manpower

With the hopes of using these resources to do more for students then send them out a random selection of mediocre job listings a few times a week.

There is no Office of Career Development in Los Angeles. That seems kind of strange, because I hear that there is a good deal of film production in that city. Wouldn't it be nice if the school had a bona fide presence on the West Coast to advocate for its students?

Well, they do. It's called Tisch Alumni West. It sounds official, doesn't it? Actually, the group is completely student run and not really affiliated with the school other than the name. Basically, a bunch of hard working alumni put the time and energy into putting on events to help each other out here in Los Angeles. They do so with minimal help from the school. That is to say, they get no money from Tisch. They do, however, get in kind contributions like cheap mailing rates, and the use of the school's web page. Which is very generous of them.

> **Subject:** Tisch West Emmy Party - We Need Your Support!
>
> **To:** "NYU Writers" <nyuwriters@yahoo.com>
>
> Dear Writers,
>
> The Tisch West Emmy Party is coming up and I want to tell you some things about it you might not know.
>
> Chandra Wilson (Grey's Anatomy), Erik Weiner (Robot Chicken), Bill D'Elia (Boston Legal), Jonathan Schmock (Real Time with Bill Maher) and Rainn Wilson (The Office) are attending. And that's just the tip of the iceberg.
>
> It's going to be a rather small crowd (they're only selling a few more tickets) and that gives you access to these writers/directors/actors in an unprecedented way. Which means, you might be able to enlist them for your upcoming readings, showcase, etc if they meet you at the party and you speak highly about your work.
>
> And here's the most important part. We, as writers, use 80% of the Tisch West funding to run our events. We benefit the most from the existence of Tisch West and we ask the most from the organization. If you're hoping to have readings or productions or development of your personal work in the future, then it's time to get involved.
>
> IT IS ESSENTIAL that the Tisch West members see that WLW members support Tisch West. Every six months, I (and now Will Matthews) go to the Council and beg for funds to keep our programming alive. If we can point to the Tisch West party lists and say – Hey, it's the writers that are showing up for or working the fundraisers – then we have a much stronger bargaining position.
>
> So please, buy a ticket and bring a friend. Your participation now ensures that WLW will continue and that your own work will have a chance to be seen.

It's nice to know that Tisch Alumni groups on the West Coast have to beg for money to keep their programming alive. I received an invitation to attend this party for $70 a ticket. I wanted to contribute, but I was wondering if it was really worth six figures plus $70 to have a chance to meet Jonathan Schmock.

LA? No Way!

In addition to the lack of funding support for any kind of West Coast assistance, the NYU List Serve rarely features job postings for Los Angeles. And that's a shame because, uh, that's where *most* of the jobs in the business...um... are.

If you don't believe me, here's a summary of all the emails I received for both the New York and LA based List serves between September 3 and October 3 2007. You've already seen the October 5 posting above. The full email includes a complete description of each job listed, but the top part gives you a good idea of what they are all about. You just take a look and see if any of these get you excited.

Subject: 10-3(NY): Job Ops
Date: Wed, 03 Oct 2007 20:19:27 -0400

```
*************************************************************
In this Alumni List Serve Correspondence you will find
the following Job Ops:

1. flash web designer - Integrated Media Solutions
2. Assistant Production Manager - Jill Platner
3. Traffic Manager - Crispin Porter + Bogusky
4. dance/drum/voice instructor - redshantree arts center
5. CityCapture - Producer/Shooter
```

Dance/Drum/Voice Instructor?

Subject: 10/2 (NY) Job Ops
Date: Tue, 02 Oct 2007 16:58:43 -0400

```
*************************************************************
In this Alumni List Serve Correspondence you will find
the following Job Ops:

1. Producer - Dame-Gramp Productions LLC
2. Program Assistant - National Dance Institute
3. Merchandise Sales Associate, Quasi World Entertainment
4. Part-time Caregiver - Clare Bassile
```

Part time caregiver?

```
Subject:   10-1(NY): Job Ops, Now for Later Ops
Date:      Mon, 01 Oct 2007 17:16:05 -0400


9/28(NY) Job Ops

*********************************************************************
In this Alumni List Serve Correspondence you will find
the following Job Ops:

1. Producer/Shooter - CityCapture
2. Executive Editor - Octagon
3. Camera Assistant, Camera Assistant, Swing Grip/Electric, Lighting
   Tech, Gaffer/Lighting Tech, Hair/Makeup, 1st Assistant Director,
   Production Designer- Rambler
4. BOX OFFICE PHONE SALES & CUSTOMER SERVICE REP - dcm, Inc.

And the following Now For Later Op:

1. auditions - workshop of a new play Spoken Insects

*********************************************************************
```

    Okay, that one had some crew positions. Phew! I thought this was going to be a total loss. Let's take a closer look:

3. Full Name of Contact Person: Ken Segna
Title: Producer
Is Contact Person a Tisch Alumna/Alumnus? No
Company Name: Rambler
Address 1: n/a
Address 2:
City: los angeles
State: California
Zip Code: 90025
Email: ▓▓▓▓▓▓▓▓▓@gmail.com
Application Instructions: Please email resume to
▓▓▓▓▓▓▓▓▓@gmail.com Thank you!
Company Description: Small production company focusing in music videos.

Wage Type: Freelance
Job Description: Production Designer $500 fee $500 budget (This is essentially 3 days of extremely simple Production Design, but we would ask the Designer to be on set the entire time. We don't have the budget for assistants). Project is a hybrid music video/documentary/short film project for Levon Helm, former drummer/singer of The Band. It will include one of Levon's legendary "Midnight Rambles" that take place in the recording studio used by Eric Clapton, Keith Richards, Dr. John and Elvis Costello. The experience should be really fun, unique and, considering Levon's place in music history, rather significant. We are looking for the following NEW YORK-based crew for the project.
a. camera assistant #1: We shoot Oct 9.
Job Qualifications: Experience as Camera Assistant for Varicam system or Sony F900.
Does this position entail working in a home-office environment? No
Start Date: 10.9.07
End Date:
Salary Information: $100/day for Oct. 9
b. camera assistant #2: We shoot Oct 9, 10, 27-30.
Job Qualifications: Experience with Varicam system or Sony F900.
Does this position entail working in a home-office environment? No
Start Date: 10.9.07
End Date:
Salary Information: $100/day for 5 days
c. Swing Grip/Electric: We shoot Oct. 9 and 27.
Job Qualifications: 1+ year experience in Swing Grip and Electric positions.
Does this position entail working in a home-office environment? No
Start Date: 10.09.07
End Date:
Salary Information: $100/day for 10/9 and 10/27
d. Lighting Tech: Dates: 10.27.07; 10.30.07
Job Qualifications: 1+ year experience in Lighting Tech positions.
Does this position entail working in a home-office environment? No
Start Date: 10.27.07
End Date:
Salary Information: $125/day for 2 shoot days
e. Gaffer/Lighting Tech: We shoot Oct 9, 10, 27-30.
Job Qualifications: 1+ year experience as Gaffer or Lighting Tech.
Does this position entail working in a home-office environment? No
Start Date: 10.9.07
End Date:
Salary Information: $150/day for 5 days
f. Hair/Makeup: We shoot Oct 9, 10, 27-30.
Job Qualifications: Multiple project experience in Hair/Makeup position

Does this position entail working in a home-office environment? No
Start Date: 10.9.07
End Date:
Salary Information: $400 kit fee for all 5 shoot days

```
g. 1st Assistant Director: We shoot Oct 9, 10, 27-30. These positions
are (modestly) paid.
Job Qualifications: Multiple projects of experience as a First
Assistant Director.
Does this position entail working in a home-office environment? No
Start Date: 10.9.07
End Date:
Salary Information: $150/day for two days
h. Production Designer: Production Designer $500 fee $500 budget (This
is essentially 3 days of extremely simple Production Design, but we
would ask the Designer to be on set the entire time. We don't have the
budget for assistants). Project is a hybrid music video/documentary/short
film project for Levon Helm, former drummer/singer of The Band. It will
include one of Levon's legendary "Midnight Rambles" that take place in
the recording studio used by Eric Clapton, Keith Richards, Dr. John
and Elvis Costello. The experience should be really fun, unique and,
considering Levon's place in music history, rather significant. We are
looking for the following NEW YORK-based crew for the project. ***We shoot
Oct 9, 10, 27-30.
Job Qualifications: Production Designer (1+ year experience) $500 fee
$500 budget This is essentially 3 days of extremely simple Production
Design, but we would ask the Designer to be on set the entire time. We
don't have the budget for assistants.
```

This production is like many of the gigs you could find on mandy.com or craigslist. Low paying, small gigs that stress the chance to network and have a good experience over making a lot of money. But hey, at least it's paying work, and that's great. If you can beat out the hundreds of other desperate Tisch grads looking for work and nail one of these positions, you may learn something.

Of course, it is NYC based. So far there hasn't been one job posting for the city of Los Angeles. Guess that town doesn't have much film work. Huh.

Oh wait! Here comes one from LA! Check it out:

Subject: 9/28 (LA) Announcement
Date: Fri, 28 Sep 2007 17:29:22 -0400

Actors Wanted for "New from NYU" Script Reading Oct 15th.

Aw, poo, that wasn't a job. Rats.

Subject: 9/26 (NY) Addendum Announcement
Date: Wed, 26 Sep 2007 18:13:24 -0400

```
Video Apprentice Positions for theatre documentary with acclaimed
actor/director - exciting project at non-profit theatre and cultural
center!

We seek student video editors/shooters or those entering the industry
who wish to make a meaningful commitment to established non-profit
professional theatre and acting conservatory. Develop your skills and
creativity under the guidance of our renowned Artistic Director and Founder,
Thurman E. Scott. The project goal is to bring the power of our
classes and programs to the public. Your work will have a lasting impact on
our theatre and community.
```

Huh. This one is funny. Is it a job? Or a chance to volunteer?

Look at the bottom, where it says how to apply:

```
Please complete an application in the "Volunteer" section at
http://www.ActorsTheatreWorkshop.com. Please specify the Video
Apprentice Program. Email us at Outreach@ActorsTheatreWorkshop.com or call
212-947-1386 ext. 0 with questions.
```

Oh, I see. . After paying a quarter of a mil for film school, you can apprentice from a real master: a non profit theater.

Awesome!

And that wasn't in LA either.

But hey, look! I found one!

Subject: 9/26(LA)Job Op
Date: Fri, 28 Sep 2007 17:29:15 -0400

```
***********************************************************
In this Alumni List Serve Correspondence you will find
the following Job Ops:

1. Filmmaker - Xtracycle

***********************************************************

1.  Full Name of Contact Person:     Kipchoge Spencer
Title:      President
Is Contact Person a Tisch Alumna/Alumnus?     No
Company Name:     Xtracycle
Address 1:     Hwy 49
Address 2:
City:     North San Juan
State:     California
Zip Code:     95960
Email:                              .com
Application Instructions:     email resume and link to work:
                             .com o
:      Email
Company Web Site:     xtracycle.com
Company Description:     Extra environmentally conscious sport utility
bicycle company. please see website for details.
Job Title:     Filmmaker
Wage Type:     Freelance
Job Description:     On October 18, 2007, the bands: The Ginger Ninjas,
and Shake Your Piece launch the"Pleasant Revolution > Tour," a rock &
roll bicycle tour spanning over 5000 > miles and playing over 90 shows
from the Sierras in N. > California, to the jungles of Chiapas, Mexico.
No > sag-wagons, and no buses hauling gear: everything, > including the
800 Watt human-powered PA System, will be hauled entirely by bicycle.
A 14-person strong > entourage makes the core, joined by bicycle and
music enthusiasts all along the route. The tour is expected to last 4
months. Ideally,we'd like a filmmaker who can go all the way to Chiapas
Job Qualifications:     Documentary & narrative experience. We're
```

  looking for hip, adventurous and energetic people. Need to be flexible,
  creative, and have strong legs.
Does this position entail working in a home-office environment?   No
Start Date: October 18, 2007
End Date: approx.February 18, 2008
Salary Information: TBD
Benefits Information: -
Please check: This is a paid position, not an internship for credit
or deferred salary position.

Ah yes, The Ginger Ninjas. This gig looks pretty cool. It ought to be. In the world according to Tisch, this one job op is the only opportunity available in Los Angeles for the entire week! Meanwhile, if you take a look at craigslist from the same day:

los angeles crew gigs classifieds - craigslist

Personal Assistant/Intern Needed for Film Director (West Hollywood)

Seeking 2 PA's for for short scene like the movie "300" Goth style (Hollywood)

LOOKING FOR MINI DV CAMERA RENTAL (LA)

video intro

Need to rent SGpro 35MM adapter...

Wed Sep 26

ARABIC TRANSLATOR

Indie film needs Small Grip Truck with or without a Grip (Los Angeles, CA)

Production intern for low budget feature (Burbank/CA)

Looking for Tony Soprano Hangout

PAs wanted (5 &110)

Paid Video Camera Intern - Experienced (Los Angeles Area)

Looking for costume help for low budget superhero film... (Los Angeles)

DP (LA)

sound equipment/lighting equipment (LA)

CAMERAMAN NEEDED FOR SPORTS/COMPETITION PILOT (HOLLYWOOD)

Casting Assistant

cheap filmmaker with cam & sound equipment needed ASAP (Mid-Wilshire)

looking to start a serious film group / production comp

CREW CALL FOR USC STUDENT FILM

Amazing PA/Casting Associate Needed ASAP (North Hollywood)

A great deal for a Filmmaker to get free gear use. (Hollywood)

looking for a producer / partner for my short

Seeking Music Video Producer!!!!! (ALL OVER)

Production Manager Needed (LA/International)

Stand In/PA

AC/FOCUS PULLER needed for Mark Twain feature documentary (Leona Valley/Pamldale, CA)

GAFFER & GRIP NEEDED FOR PSA SPOT (Westside)

EVENT COMPANY SEEKING PROFESSIONAL PEOPLE (HOLLYWOOD)

PA needed for ultra low budget feature

Discovery Channel seeking builders/designers for new project.

INDIE FILM INTERNSHIP (West LA)

Sound Editor Wanted (Hollywood)

PA's Needed this weekend (Redondo Beach)

PRODUCTION PARTNERS (Hollywood)

NEED EFX MAKE-UP ARTIST (So.cal)

Interns & Volunteers wanted JULES VERNE FILM FESTIVAL

Production Assistant AFI Film Festival (Hollywood)

Editors needed ASAP (LA)

FILM COMPANY SEEKS TALENTED INTERNS!

MUSIC VIDEO EDITOR (BURBANK,CA)

RECEPTION/CLIENT SERVICE (Santa Monica)

Editor Needed

Experienced Co-Producer Needed (Hollywood)

WARDROBE SUPERVISOR / ASSISTANT COSTUME DESIGNER (LOS ANGELES / MEXICO)

Musicians/Composers Needed for Rock Musical

Production Team in all Departments needed 4 short.

Gaffer needed for faith based feature

Production Company Seeks Script Readers (Hollywood)

Seeking dynamic PRODUCTION COORDINATOR (Los Angeles (westside))

Assistant Director Needed (Morocco)

Varicam camera operator (LA)

los angeles crew gigs classifieds - craigslist

Need AUDIO TECH for feature-length documentary - Mark Twain (Leona Valley/Palmdale, CA)

Storyboard Artist Wanted

Studio Teacher needed for Children's Video Shoot (Los Angeles)

GORILLA BUDGET & SCHEDULING SOFTWARE

Intern Needed - Busy Production Company (Sherman Oaks)

Editor needed for Re-cut shortfilm (Hollywood)

Camera operator with scuba gear / experience needed...

GRIP DRIVER NEEDED - Must have Class A license (Los Angeles, CA)

Someone cheap to do some cast and crew deals (Hollywood)

DP with own Sony HVR-Z1U (West Los Angeles)

Need editor or D.P. with JVC HD GY110U camera to capture asap!! (studio city)

Need a Studio in Santa Monica (SANTA MONICA)

The Idea Factory is Looking for Reality Show Ideas! img

Writer wanted: Award winning director looking for short film scripts (anywhere)

Wardrobe - Costume Supervisor Needed ASAP

Gorilla Film Budget & Scheduling Software (Los Angeles)

producer's assitant (LA)

Camera Operators (L.A. & O.C.)

Sound Engineer (Long Beach)

Sound Engineer (Long Beach)

EDITOR for FINAL CUT PRO needed OCT 21ST (Long Beach/LA)

Tue Sep 25

1st Assistant Camera (Southern California)

Wardrobe Assistant Needed (Los Angeles)

Transpo driver

Crafty Service

And now, back to Tisch. Let's look at September 25:

```
Subject:   9-25(NY): Job Ops, Now For Later Ops, Alumni Announcements
Date:      Tue, 25 Sep 2007 15:20:23 -0400


*****************************************************************
In this Alumni List Serve Correspondence you will find the following
 Job Ops:

1. Administrative Assistant - Mendola LTD
2. Camera Operator - Felix Rodriguez Films
3. Videographer/DP - TV Guide Magazine
4. Writer - Third Way Productions
5. Programmer Analyst - Hart Systems
6. Film & Theatre Company Assistant - EarthHart Productions

The following Now For Later Ops:

1. P.A.'s needed in all departments for low-budget independent dramatic
   feature

and the following Alumni Announcement:

1. new weekly television show titled "Brooklyn Kino" on Brooklyn
   Community Access Television
*****************************************************************
```

Six listings. Not bad. Camera Op, Videographer, Writer. Almost up to snuff with craigslist.

Of course, craigslist is free. And there are postings every day.

And you're paying $390 a month in loans for this List Serve, which is sent out sporadically a few times a month.

Let's take a closer look at this Administrative Assistant position. That sounds promising...

Company Name: Mendola LTD
Address 1: 420 Lexinton Ave
Address 2: PH
City: New York
State: New York
Zip Code: 10170
Email: ▇▇▇▇▇▇▇.com
Application Instructions: Please email Cover Letter and Resume
Company Web Site: mendolaart.com
Company Description: Mendola Artists is a small company, in business
 for over 40 years, that represents illustrators from all over the world.
 Our illustrators create high profile images for the advertising,
 editorial, packaging and publishing markets.
Job Title: Administrative Assistant
Wage Type: Full-time
Job Description: We are looking for a friendly and organized individual
 to handle ! the administrative duties of a small but busy office.
 Everyday respons ibilities include answering a multi-line phone system,
 managing the invoicing, collections and monthly sales reports and
 maintaining the files and records of the company. Additionally, this person
 will be responsible for scanning, color correcting and uploading images to
 websites, assisting the sales reps with gathering artist materials and
 portfolios, supervising the messenger on staff and processing all
 internet shipping. Other administrative and organizational tasks always pop
 up during the course of a day so the person in this position must be
 able to multi-task and work with a flexible attitude.
Job Qualifications: The applicant must be extremely computer savvy and
 have excellent writing and communication skills. Knowledge of both
 Windows and Mac OS, MS Office- Word, Excel, and Outlook- are a must.
 Experience using a scanner, Quickbooks, and Photoshop are highly desired.
Does this! position entail working in a home-office environment? No
Start Date: ASAP
End Date:
Salary Information: 25,000-30,000
Benefits Information: Medical after Probation Period
Please check: This is a paid position, not an internship for credit or
 deferred salary position.

Hmmm. Interesting. This reminds me of something. Something very special. Can't guess what it is? Good, it's a surprise! I'll show it to you on the next page...

Remember this awesome bar graph!? That's the surprise!

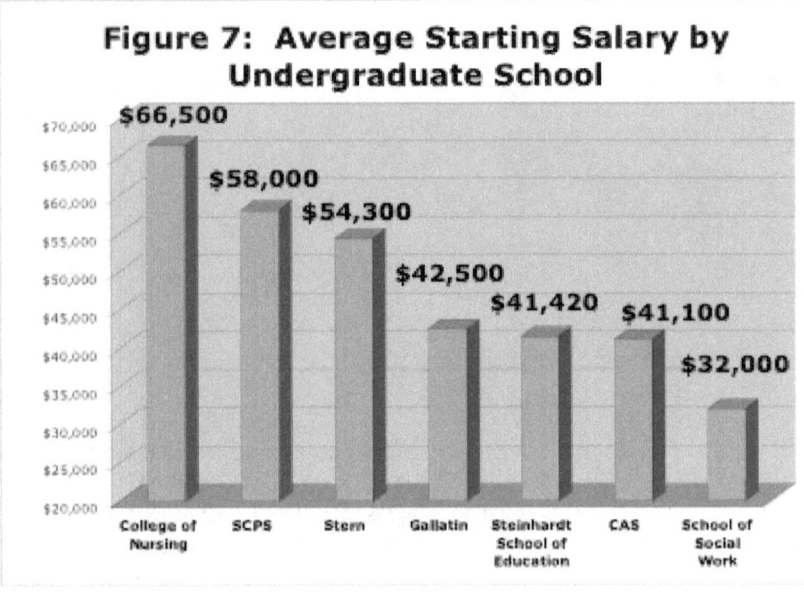

Figure 7: Average Starting Salary by Undergraduate School

If this posting for a job as an Administrative Assistant paying $25,000 to $30,000 a year is the type of opportunity Tisch offers its grads, then I understand why Tisch was left out of the school's comprehensive report on average starting salary. They simply didn't have enough room at the bottom of the bar graph.

Bar graphs are forgiving and beautiful; the grim reality is not.

Unless you want to starve, at some point you will probably have to find an office job, at least a temp one. The bad news is that office jobs outside of the entertainment industry pay much better than jobs inside the entertainment industry.

Example? I make $17 an hour temping in the HR Department of a company that makes teeth whitening products. The same day I receive an email about a temp job working as a receptionist at a post-production house, for $10 an hour going to $13 in 3 months when the job becomes permanent. With the hopes it will lead to something in editing. Keep those fingers crossed!

Or, I get an email like this one. Working for a company that represents illustrators making $12 an hour. (Or, 15 minutes of a class at NYU).

Across the board, people hiring for jobs related to entertainment in any way tend to pay much less. It's simply because of all the glitz and glamour surrounding the business. People are so starry eyed and desperate to work near movies or entertainment in any way that they will accept lower than tolerable work wages, and so it lowers the bar for everybody. I have never seen more listings for jobs paying under $30,000 a year than on the Tisch List Serve.

Here's some more bad news. Employers don't care where you went to school. The ratio of how irrelevant where you attended college is, of if you attended school at all, to how important it is perceived to be by most unsuspecting parents, teachers, and students, is so skewed that it delights Satan and makes Jesus cry.

Prospective employers in any field are primary concerned with your *work experience*. That's why you are so far behind the 18 year old who has 4 years of employment on his resume versus your 4 years of sitting in classrooms listening to Cable Ace Award winners.

Imagine you are the Production Manager of a movie. You need a Gaffer. Are you going to hire somebody who has been hanging lights on other movies for 4 years, or some kid who just graduated school and has never worked in a professional environment?

Same thing applies to the world of business. And that's why you are only eligible for *entry level* positions. Like the one listed above.

And your boss will probably be younger than you.

Think I am being overly dramatic? Check out this little blurb from page 231 of the first edition of "Film School Confidential".

> "So, you've got your degree and have made the big move to Los Angeles only to find your door is not being broken down by agents and producers. Once you have resigned yourself to this, you will be ready to join the ranks of the gainfully, if not happily, employed. The next fact you need to resign yourself to is that whatever job you wind up in, you probably could have gotten that job without an M.F.A. In fact, it is quite possible that you will find yourself working as a veritable slave to someone younger, less skilled, and less educated than yourself."

I'll let you in on a little secret. It's called the UTA Job Posting. It's a super classified list of jobs in the entertainment biz compiled by the United Talent Agency. I get copies in my email from an actress friend. But recently, Tisch started sending out copies of UTA on its list serve as well. These are some of the most coveted positions to work with A list people in the top level of the biz.

Now, take a look at this first posting:

```
Second assistant needed for busy film producer. Candidates must have
bachelor's degree; previous industry experience (particularly
 production)
preferred. Must be detail-oriented, organized and have excellent
communication skills. Duties include rolling calls, scheduling, filing
 and
office runs. Will start end of June. Please send resume and cover
 letter
to ███████████████████████████    6/6
```

What's this? Bachelor's degree required? But Seth, you said that employers don't care where we went to school!

They don't. All it says is Bachelor's Degree. It could be from NYU or a state school in Montana. And this posting is the exception to the rule. Here's some of the more typical listings:

Producer Robert Simonds (Pink Panther, Yours, Mine & Ours, Billy Madison)
seeks a 1st assistant. Candidates must be motivated, extremely detail oriented, resourceful and thick skinned. Must have previous desk experience in the film industry. This is a demanding job, but an excellent
opportunity for someone committed to a career in development/producing. Please email resume and cover letter to ▓▓▓▓▓@yahoo.com. 6/6

Production company with a studio deal seeks an assistant to the CE.
Person
will also function as a 2nd to the Chairman when necessary. Looking for a
motivated, self-starter with a positive attitude, strong organizational skills and impeccable follow through. Interest in development and some industry experience preferred. Please email resume and cover letter to ▓▓▓▓▓@yahoo.com. 6/6

CEO of a motion picture production / distribution company and private charitable foundation seeks Executive Assistant. Must possess at least 2
years experience as an Administrative Assistant/Personal Assistant, organizational ability, exceptional verbal and written communication skills. Correspondence, scheduling, and coordinating personal/professional
activities, including travel. Personality, maturity, and experience at a
literary agency and/or as a personal assistant is a plus. Email resume and
salary requirements to ▓▓▓@samuelgoldwyn.com. No phone calls please. 6/6

Katapult Film Sales is seeking a full-time sales assistant. Looking for someone with one year or more of industry experience, history at an agency
preferable. Must be independently hard working, detail-oriented, and eager
to learn about the independent/foreign world of film. Duties to include corresponding with clients, accounting, communicating with film festivals,
and preparing for film markets. Work environment is friendly, much opportunity for learning and growth. Please forward resumes to David at ▓▓▓▓▓▓▓▓▓▓.com. 6/6

Nothing about college.

Just previous work experience.

So I guess if you'd skipped school and just gone to work, you couldn't apply for that first job. But you could apply for these 4.

Let's see if there are any more like this...

```
Assistant position available for a producer/manager at Lighthouse
Entertainment, a successful boutique company in Beverly Hills.  Tasks
include rolling calls, handling press requests, taking appointments,
sending out submissions and script coverage.  Huge opportunity to learn a
lot about producing and talent representation.  Must be proficient with
Mac, Microsoft Word, Excel, iPhoto, Final Draft.  Knowledge of Entourage a
huge plus.  Please e-mail resumes to ███████████@yahoo.com or fax
███████████.  6/6

High-end management company looking for assistant.  Agency, management or
casting experience required.  Multi-tasking, attention to detail, and
desire to pursue a career in management a must.  Please email resumes and
cover letters ASAP to ███████████████████  6/6

Two reality television Executive Producers are seeking a savvy,
detail-oriented, team-players with a genuine passion for reality TV.  This
job is tailored for individuals with a strong work ethic, a comedic
outlook, and a desire for growth and diversity.  Standard industry hours
and salary apply, position begins approximately June 11.  Email your resume
(with references) to: ███████████████████gmail.com.  6/6

Senior Talent Manager seeks experienced 2nd assistant to roll calls,
schedule meetings and coordinate submissions.  Applicant must be smart,
resilient, detail-oriented and able to multi-task in a fast-paced
environment.  Full time position, but applicants seeking part-time work are
also encouraged to apply.  Send resume as Word attachment to
███████████████████████████.com.  6/6

Assistant to Talent Manager - Must have entertainment experience,
preferably at an agency, management company or casting office.  General
office duties including answering phones, filing, scheduling appointments,
breakdowns, script reading and coverage.  Great work environment.  Please
```

Okay, here's 5 more listings that say nothing about college.

Oh, and see that that third one from the bottom? The one that says "standard industry hours and salary apply"? That's code for: "long hours and shitty pay".

If you apply to any of these jobs you are basically applying to be "Lloyd" from "Entourage". Somebody's lackey. Bitch. Assistant. Making chicken scratch. These are the most sought after jobs in the business, with the promise of networking and advancement.

```
Top notch assistant needed immediately for A list Director/Producer.
 Must
have minimum of 2 years working for A list Director in busy
 professional
office, excellent communication skills, excellent technical skills
(computers, cell phones, some camera equipment), on set experience,
 thick
 skin, and be organized and efficient. Full time position with overtime
 and
some weekend work. You will be one assistant on a team of 2 with shared
and separate responsibilities. Salary based on experience. Cover letter
and resume to ███████@hotmail.com. 6/6
```

"Thick skin" is code for "be prepared to work with an asshole".

Honestly, why would you need a college degree to assist somebody? Was there some class in college on assisting? I guess they could charge you $4,592 to learn how to order a latte.

If you start at the bottom, work hard and pay your dues, you will be successful. But why did you need to pay $200,000 to an academic institution to learn nothing and start from the bottom?

These jobs are on the Producing/Development end of things. To be a Gaffer or Grip or Director of Photography you need to just start getting your hands dirty and work on as many productions as possible. Again, learn by doing, not by sitting.

Now, if you actually went to NYU Film with the intention of making your own movies, you should just skip these jobs altogether. Get a good job that pays well outside of film and use your nights and weekends to network and work on your own projects.

Unless, of course, you want to pursue one of these exciting opportunities:

Subject: 9/21(NY) Job Ops

Date: Fri, 21 Sep 2007 21:13:29 -0400

```
*****************************************************************
```
In this Alumni List Serve Correspondence you will find
the following Job Ops:

1. IT/Programming Manager - iEARN-USA
2. Thinning Hair Actress/Model/Spokesperson - Cobalt Balloon
3. Concept Artist, 2D Animation - Kindness of Strangers Productions
4. Open Call - The Awesome 80's Prom Cabaret
```
*****************************************************************
```

or

Subject: 9-20 (NY): Job Ops, Alumni Announcements, Now For Later

Date: Thu, 20 Sep 2007 17:07:14 -0400

```
*****************************************************************
```
In this Alumni List Serve Correspondence you will find
the following Job Ops:

1. Website Assitant/Production Editor - INFORM, INC
2. Webzine designer/developer sought for new travel magazine - Big
   World Multimedia

The Following Now For Later Ops:
1. casting female lead - Independent web pilot

And the following Alumni announcement:

1. casting call

Or...

Subject: 9/10 (NY) Job Ops and Announcements

Date: Mon, 10 Sep 2007 16:26:29 -0400

```
*****************************************************************
```
In this Alumni List Serve Correspondence you will find
the following Job Ops:

1. Receptionist - Epoch Films
2. System Analyst - Morgan Stanley
3. Online Media Supervisor - Special Ops Media
4. Media Planner - Special Ops Media
5. Art Director - Special Ops Media
6. Sound Recording Instructor - New York Film Academy

And the following Announcements:

1. Show Announcement - Stone Soup Theatre
2. Show Announcement - Emergency Contraception the Musical

Or...

Subject: 7/4 (NY) Job Ops part III

Date: Tue, 04 Sep 2007 16:50:38 -0400

```
************************************************************
In this Alumni List Serve Correspondence you will find
the following Job Ops:

1. Mandarin-English Translator - VBS IPTV LLC
2. Male VO Talent - Acoustiguide
3. DP/Cinematographer - WIKA LLC
4. African American Male and Female VO Talent - Acoustiguide
5. Interaction Designer - Fox Interactive Media
************************************************************
```

And finally:

Subject: 7/4 (LA) Job Ops

Date: Tue, 04 Sep 2007 11:53:54 -0400

```
************************************************************
In this Alumni List Serve Correspondence you will find
the following Job Ops:

1. Freelance Writer - UGO Networks
2. Junior Lighting Designer - Francis Krahe & Associates Inc
```

Now doesn't it feel good to be in the inner circle of the industry?

Afterword

I enrolled in film school to learn how to make feature films. But it wasn't until 7 years after graduation that I finally set about doing just that.

Here's a little storyboard summary of the "Breaking Balls" trailer:

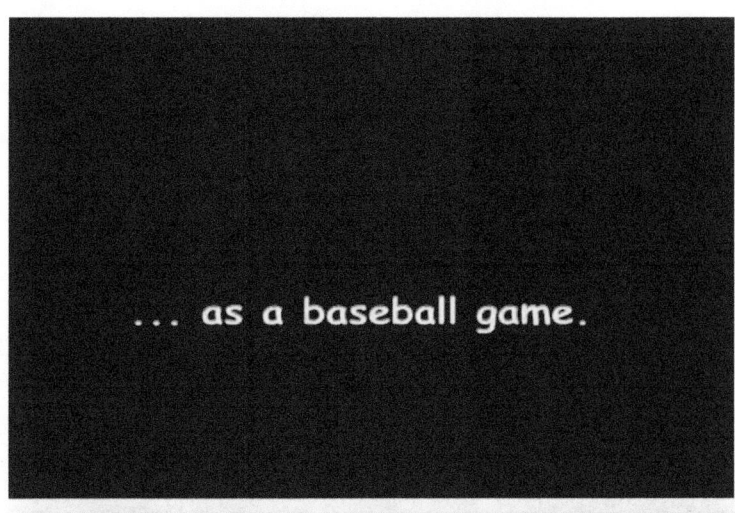

TIGERS
TCR 08:14:29:26

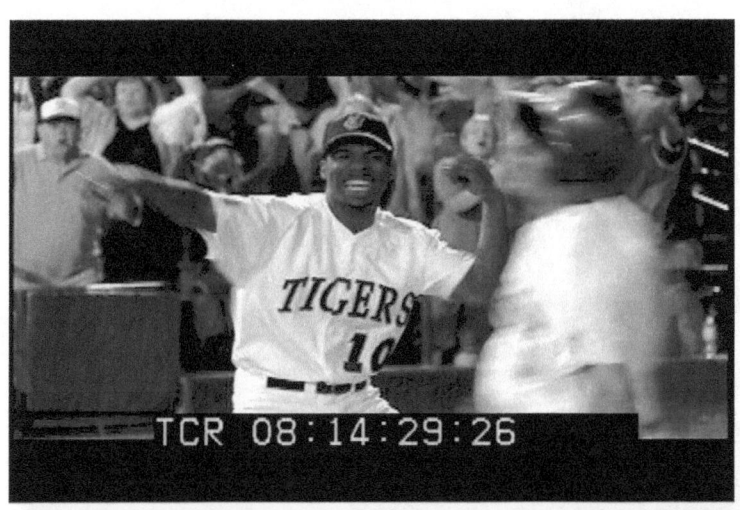

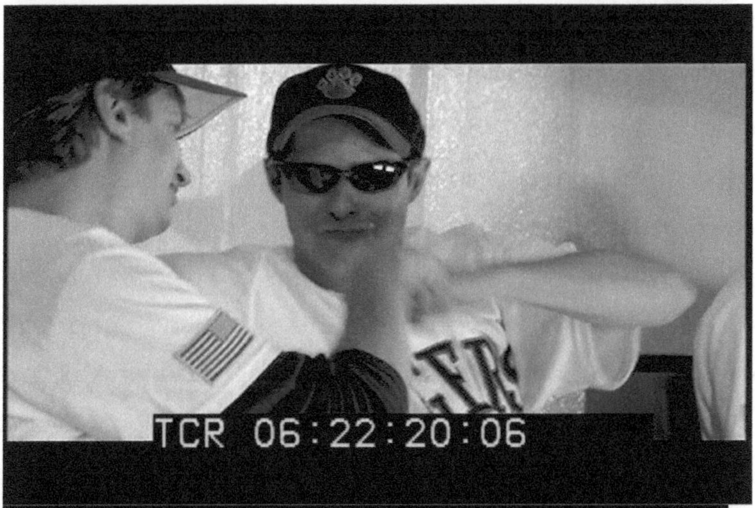
TCR 06:22:20:06

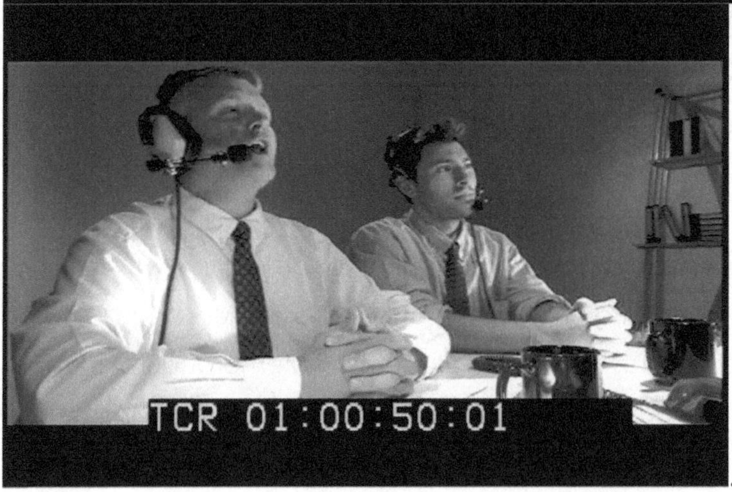
TCR 01:00:50:01

You can see the full trailer on You Tube at:
http://www.youtube.com/watch?v=dkJbESS1eNo

The song in the background is called "Let Go" by a great Powerpop band from Buffalo called Bensin. Check them out at http://www.myspace.com/bensin.

Now, maybe you are wondering where you can find 'Breaking Balls"? Well, unfortunately, you can't. The movie isn't done. I'd set out raising money for the $190,000 budget in 3 months. A difficult goal. By networking within the local business community, I found two wonderful investors. One cut me a check for $20,000 and the other for $10,000.

$30,000 was a great start, but it wasn't enough to meet the $80,000 minimum budget. Or the ultra low, profit sharing $52,000 budget. So even though I'd raised the $30,000, I couldn't use any of it.

My Grandma gave me my inheritance early. It was roughly $15,000. The last of the savings after college. I used $5,000 to pay the attorneys for the Private Placement Memorandum, the document registered with the Securities & Exchange Commission that's necessary to legally receive investor money. Truthfully, PPM's usually cost anywhere from $10,000 to $50,000 depending on the size of the investment, so I really got a deal. But it's kind of hard to feel good about that when you are holding a stack of papers in your hand instead of your movie.

I used the other $10,000 to shoot as much as possible. Everybody worked for less than their day rate with the understanding they would be reimbursed when the money was raised. We were using tens of thousands of dollars worth of camera and grip equipment. We had access to a beautiful AAA baseball stadium. I went on the Radio and TV to recruit extras. People showed up, excited and enthusiastic. Everybody had a great time.

I absolutely loved directing. Standing in the middle of the set, working with my Assistant Director on which shots to get, coming up with new ones on the spot... yelling "action"... it was a blast! It was what I'd dreamed of doing 7 years earlier.

At around 11 PM each night I handed my friend Jessica my dwindling credit card and she generously picked up food for everyone. Watching the cast and crew enjoy some tasty burgers and fries after working so hard, I really swelled up with gratitude. I was glad I could at least give them something good to eat after all of the time and energy they had put into making this silly little movie.

We had 2 great shooting nights at Frontier Field before the money was gone. I cut the footage I had into a trailer and tried to raise more. But soon the Fall had turned to winter and it began to snow. Since the movie revolved around baseball, it would have to wait another year. I couldn't wait another 7 months without doing anything.

So I moved to Los Angeles. I still had $30,000 in the bank, and 2 investors who believed in the movie. I figured I would do the same thing in LA that I had done in Rochester. Join a networking business group and start talking to as many people as I could.

I'm confident the money will be raised and the movie will be made. But I can't help but think back to last year's shoot. After all, I had the script. The crew. The talent. The locations. The vision. The energy. An entire community enthusiastically ready and willing to contribute their time and energy. Just like when I was back in high school, shooting little movies.

The only thing I did not have... was the money.

I'd spent it all on NYU.

I thought I did a pretty good job trying to get the movie made this first time around considering that nobody in film school talked about money, or fundraising, or working out deals with your crew, or Private Placement Memorandums, or distribution.

When I enrolled in the school, I was under the impression that there was a vast network of professionals in place to help recent graduates produce and finance their films. This just isn't the case. Instead, I had to start from square one, as if I had never attended one of the country's most prestigious film programs. Our classes weren't even focused on the craft of making feature films. All this time and energy was spent making a few very expensive shorts.

The dream of every film student is to make a short film that wins them attention at festivals. But then what? The only logical reason to make a short film is to establish the credibility to raise money to make a feature. Nobody makes a career out of shooting short films. But you've just spent the same amount of money it would have cost to go out and make a feature on 4 years of making a couple of shorts, which you hope you can use to get you the money to make a feature.

It just doesn't make any sense.

Those 2 nights at Frontier Field were fantastic. I hope that if you are inspired to make movies, you have a chance to experience the same thrill and satisfaction of directing your own project and working with such a generous and dedicated group of professionals. I hope you have the chance to not only be creative, but to make a living being creative. Filmmaking is a business. Those who control the money control the movie.

Once you enter the fray of independent filmmaking, your primary struggles will always be financial. Back in Rochester, I met a woman who produced "Outside Providence" and "The Door in the Floor". I was trying to raise $250,000 to make "Breaking Balls" (ideally we'd have an extra chunk of change for marketing). She was selling points in her new movie at $250,000 *a share*, trying to raise $3 million in addition to $2 million she'd already raised.

It doesn't matter if you're working on a low budget indie, or a Hollywood blockbuster, everybody listens to the money. Don't be so quick to take out loans, go in debt, and give up your college savings without considering exactly what you are investing in… and what you could be using it for instead.

Society trains us to save for college so blindly, with no real assessment of the value of the education. I hope this book has given you an idea of what kind of value you can expect if you matriculate through NYU Film. Or any other 4 year, "name" film program.

You might be scared by the prospect of not having a college degree. If so, I suggest that you check out the book "Real World Careers: Why College is NOT the Only Path to Becoming Rich" by Betsy Cummings. Ms. Cummings is an award winning business writer for the New York Times, Adweek, Smart Money, and other business magazines. The book is a detailed account of the many careers that don't require a degree, and many successful people who never went to college.

In the meantime, reflect on this passage from page 297 of the 2nd edition of "Film School Confidential."

> "In many cases, you won't want to include your MFA on your resume. Ironically, an MFA in film will probably help you more outside of Hollywood than inside...... People in the industry have a preconception that MFA students think they are better than everyone else, are liable to not take their jobs seriously, and if put into positions where they can communicate with powerful people, might promote their own careers to the detriment of their employers. (It bears mentioning that this preconception is not always inaccurate).
>
> Several people we know, who have MFAs in film and work in film and television production do not include their degrees on their resumes. They found that when that was included on their resumes, they were rarely hired. It was only when they removed the MFA from their resumes that they started getting work."

And they are talking about a *Master's* degree.

Consider the financial repercussions before applying to film school, or any college for that matter. Your parents may have put aside a large amount of money for your education. You may never again have an opportunity like this. You may never again have access to this volume of capital.

Do you really want to spend it on slideshows and black and white silent movies? Do you really want to spend it arguing with your professors for the right to shoot a movie? Do you really want to spend it on a degree that has no discernable value in your field, and may even end up being a liability?

If not, I have a few options for you to consider.

The first is to get an apprenticeship. That is, find a working producer, writer, or director to learn from directly. That's how it was done in the old days. If you're not sure how, I'd suggest checking out www.film-connection.com. The service is not free, but it costs substantially less than film school and gets you right into the real world of filmmaking.

Secondly, take Dov Siemen's Two Day Filmmaking course. http://dovsimensfilmschool.com. The class is one tenth the cost of a course at NYU, and it covers filmmaking from start to finish. This course has been taken by Quentin Tarantino, Guy Ritchie, Christopher Nolan, and many others.

Thirdly, check out community colleges like Los Angeles Community College (www.lacc.edu) or Glendale Community College (www.glendale.edu). And definitely, *definitely* check out Orange County Community College and Santa Monica Community College. Hol-ee-shit. This OC program knocked my socks off. Seriously. Check out their schedule of fees. Now check out their facilities. This program is streamlined to get its graduates working in the business, and it costs practically nothing. For Southern Cali it's unreal, much better than USC.

By the way, I know just as many pissed off USC grads who felt they got ripped off by their school as I do NYU Grads. Both schools should share the same motto. "NYU and USC: Where egos are built and wallets are broken."

A friend of mine took me to the Orange Coast college campus. The State of California just received a bond to further endow their already kick ass Community College System. You have got to check out their website.

Film / Video Facilities and Equipment

Orange Coast College is a top notch Film/Video production and post-production facility. The facilities include a fully-digital TV studio, equipped with 16x9 wide-screen cameras, state-of-the-art computer-controlled lighting system, teleprompting, and professional digitial switching and audio; a large screening room with a digital sound production facilty for sound effects, dialog, and final mixing; 16mm film cameras and on-location, film and video production equipment; Sony® HDV, digital and analog field video production equipment, professional lighting and accessories; you provide the imagination.

Post-production editing on Avid® Media Composer, Avid® DV Xpress, FinalCut Pro®, digital audio editing on Fairlight MFX3® and Digidesign ProTools.

Facilities and equipment are constantly being upgraded to meet the demands of the rapidly changing film/video industry.

Student Technical Director at the Console

Students Working on a Holiday Design Show

The Screening Room

Students in the Engineering Room

They have HD Cameras, a newly remodeled $1 million facility complete with TV Studio and 16 mm film cameras. Most of the same stuff found at Tisch and USC. Even if you're a non-resident it's way cheaper than one of the big schools, and more practical. It's hard to feel ripped off when you are paying Twenty Dollars a unit. THE TUITION FOR THE ENTIRE CIRRICULUM IS LESS THAN THE COST OF ONE CLASS AT TISCH.

B'GUH!?!!

2701 Fairview Rd., P.O. Box 5005, Costa Mesa, CA 92628-5005 • orangecoastcollege.edu • Robert Dees, President

Student Budgets
2007-2008

9-Month Budget - Full Time   ($20/unit enrollment fee)

	At Home	Away
Resident Tuition & Fees	$618	$618
Non-Resident Fee	$4,368	$4,368
Room & Board	$3,978	$9,936
Books & Supplies	$1,422	$1,422
Transportation	$990	$1,098
Personal	$2,898	$2,520
Computer	$900	$900
Total Resident	**$10,806**	**$16,464**
Total Non-Resident	**$15,174**	**$20,862**

9-Month Budget - Less than half time   ($20 unit enrollment fee)

	At Home	Away
Resident Tuition & Fees	$618	$618
Non-Resident Fee	$4,368	$4,368
Books & Supplies	$1,422	$1,422
Transportation	$990	$1,098
Computer	$900	$900
Total Resident	**$3,930**	**$4,038**
Total Non-Resident	**$8,298**	**$8,406**

* Fees are subject to change.
** Non-resident Tuition Fee is $156/unit + enrollment fees.
*** Based on the average of 14 units/semester, $20 a unit, $14 Health Fee, and $15 Student Service Charge/semeste
****(Summer health fee is $11).

http://www.orangecoastcollege.edu/academics/divisions/visual_arts/film_and_video/

A lot of people rush through a 2 year program with the hopes of being admitted to a more expensive 4 year program so they can earn their Bachelor's Degree.

DON'T.

YOU DO NOT NEED IT.

IT IS A WASTE OF TIME.

IT WILL NEVER BE WORTH THE PRICE.

NOBODY CARES WHERE YOU WENT TO SCHOOL.

Okay fourth suggestion: read a ton of books on filmmaking. They are everywhere. At Barnes and Noble, Amazon.com. The one I like best is "How to Make a Feature Film for Under $10,000 (And Not Go to Jail)" by Brett Stern. The author is witty and humble, like me, and he knows his shit. "Feature Filmmaking for Used Car Prices" by Rich Schmidt is also good. "Shot by Shot" by Steven D. Katz gets the basics. And it bears repeating that you should check out http://acceptable.tv/tutorials to see some hysterically informative vids featuring Jack Black. For pure inspiration check out "Rebel Without a Crew" by Robert Rodriguez.

Finally, get on www.mandy.com., www.entertaimentcareers.net, and www.craigslist.com and look for internships and low budget movies that need help. For temp work in the film business, go to www.comaragency.com and www.eleventhhourent.com. For apartments in LA check out www.westsiderentals.com. And if you're married but want to engage in a discreet affair, try www.ashleymadison.com. That's not particularly relevant to your job or apartment search, but I heard about it on the radio this morning and thought it sounded interesting.

The worst thing film school can do to you is give you a "film school" vibe. People in the business hate this. It's when you send off the air of "I went to film school, therefore I am somehow smarter and better than you." I've heard one story of a guy on set of a popular network TV show who boasted his prestigious school in the form of a window sticker and got his car egged.

I know it may be stupid for a know it all like me to be dissing harsh on know it alls. By my own reckoning, if I were to step foot on a film set I would be mercilessly stoned with stale bagels until death. But consider this. As you prepare to graduate, everybody older than you thinks they know it all. Your parents, your teachers, your guidance counselors, they are all pushing you like mad to go to college. They think they know it's your only chance to be successful.

But do they really know? When was the last time they were in school, or had to look for a job?

Talk to people in the field you wish to pursue. Talk to recent graduates. You'll get a better idea of the reality, not the fantasy. Yes, it would be nice if you could go to school and get a great job in your field and live happily ever after. But if you surf "facebook", you'll find an alarming number of groups with silly titles like "I have an English Degree and I will be living in a box." It's kind of funny, but kind of true. Thousands of young people are digging themselves into a huge financial ditch, sometimes hundreds of thousands of dollars, to earn degrees in English, History, Philosophy… and even Film. They know they are doing it, but they do it anyway. Like they don't have any other choice.

But you do. You have plenty of options.

Weight them carefully.

Have some adventures, and good luck!

www.ingramcontent.com/pod-product-compliance
Lightning Source LLC
Chambersburg PA
CBHW020949230426
43666CB00005B/245